SENTENCES
CHILDREN USE

SENTENCES
CHILDREN USE

PAULA MENYUK

RESEARCH MONOGRAPH NO. 52

THE M.I.T. PRESS

CAMBRIDGE, MASSACHUSETTS, AND LONDON, ENGLAND

372.61
M529

To *Curtis, Diane, and Eric*

Foreword

This is the fifty-second volume in the M.I.T. Research Monograph Series published by the M.I.T. Press. The objective of this series is to contribute to the professional literature a number of significant pieces of research, larger in scope than journal articles but normally less ambitious than finished books. We believe that such studies deserve a wider circulation than can be accomplished by informal channels, and we hope that this form of publication will make them readily accessible to research organizations, libraries, and independent workers.

Howard W. Johnson

Preface

The acquisition and development of language in children has recently been the subject of a great deal of psychological, linguistic, and neurophysiological speculation, and a modest amount of relevant experimentation. One might ask why both conditions exist. From the viewpoint of the linguist, an understanding of the way in which language is acquired and develops would give further evidence of the validity of a theory about the structure of language. It would be logical to suppose that a child, in understanding and producing a language, uses the structural aspects of the language which the linguist might use to characterize it. The psychologist and neurophysiologist would like to understand the nature and behavior of the organism that acquires a system of communication that is unique in kind from that of all other animals and the nature of the system of communication that is acquired. On the other hand, for the linguist and psychologist, the basic task of eliciting information from the child about what structural aspects of the language he is using to understand and produce utterances is a difficult one, and neurophysiological experimentation is restricted by the fact that subjects, by definition, must be human.

In addition to theoretical interest, there has recently been a rebirth of concern and interest on the part of researchers in child development, education, and speech pathology, in obtaining a better understanding of the processes of language acquisition and development. This renewed interest has been fostered by the results of linguistic studies which use a generative model of grammar to describe language. Although research to date has merely begun to explore insightful questions about language acquisition, the results of this experimentation have shown that many previous notions about language and its use are not descriptive of the processes of language acquisition and development. They, therefore, could not successfully be applied in the teaching of language or the modification of linguistic behavior. Further, these results indicate the vast and rich information that experimentation from this point of view can bring.

Therefore, it seems appropriate at this time to present a summary of research that has been carried out, using some of the techniques of experimental psychology within the framework of a generative model of grammar, which describes the sentences children use at various stages of development. After using this framework to establish what is acquired and used one can then ask how it is acquired and used.

The introductory chapter discusses the possible goals of descriptions of language acquisition and development and the experimental approaches which have been and can be used to attain these goals. In large part, what follows are the results of some experiments which describe the structure of the sentences children produce and comprehend from age 2 to 7 years. Most of the research that is reported is concerned with the acquisition and development of syntactic rules, although children's acquisition of phonological and semantic rules is touched upon, primarily to indicate how little has been done in those areas of grammar acquisition. In addition, the results of some studies comparing the linguistic behavior of children developing language normally and children developing language in a deviant manner are presented. An attempt is made to indicate how systematic comparisons of the use of language by normal-speaking children and children whose language usage deviates in differing ways from the norm may lead us to a better understanding of the correlations between language use and the psychological functions which underly this use.

Although some relationships between the structure of the language and observable behavior have been established by experimentation, there are many aspects of this relationship which remain unexplored. Therefore, frequent indications will be given of what the author believes is our present state of knowledge and where further fruitful investigation may lie.

Grateful acknowledgement is given to the administration and teachers of the Brookline, Massachusetts, school system and recreational program for their cooperation in the gathering of the data. I am particularly grateful to the children whose sentences were used. The research was greatly assisted by courses taken at Massachusetts Institute of Technology and discussions with members of the Linguistics and Speech Communication groups in the

Research Laboratory of Electronics; in particular, Professors Noam Chomsky, Morris Halle, and Kenneth N. Stevens.

Most of the research for this book was conducted while the author was a postdoctoral fellow (MF-8768 from the National Institute of Mental Health, Public Health Service) and a staff member at the Research Laboratory of Electronics, Massachusetts Institute of Technology. The research is supported in part by the National Institute of Health (Grant 5R01 NB-04332-05) and by the U.S. Air Force Cambridge Research Laboratories, Office of Aerospace Research Contract No. AF 19 (628)-5661.

Cambridge, Massachusetts   Paula Menyuk

Contents

SENTENCES
CHILDREN USE

1 Some Theoretical Considerations

Various disciplines express interest and concern in the task of describing the processes of language acquisition and development, but for differing reasons. Each discipline has its own goals, methods of procedures, and particular prejudices. Each discipline suggests with varying degrees of determination that its theoretical models of the process and explanation of the observed or collected data are the most comprehensive and adequate. Despite their having conflicting views of procedure and explanation, all of these disciplines have contributed to a clarification of the processes of speech perception and production in terms of both their theories and their experimental techniques. It is now the task of those who wish to describe the processes of language acquisition and development to determine the goals and approaches which seem to offer the most promise in obtaining both a description and an explanation of these processes.

1.1 The Goals of a Description of Language Acquisition and Development

The goal of linguistic descriptions is to describe the linguistic competence of the language user. That is, linguists attempt to describe all the generalizations about the language that the native speaker has knowledge of and uses to derive the meaning of an utterance and to express intended meaning. This knowledge or competence is reformulated by writing the grammars of languages which consist of structural descriptions of the possible sentences of the language. These are models of possible sentences, not descriptions of sentences in a language corpus.

In most instances the linguist uses his own knowledge of the language to derive structural descriptions of the possible sentences. He will, on occasion, test "borderline" sentences by asking for a consensus about the goodness, that is, grammaticalness, of particular sentence exemplars. When attempting to derive the grammar of an unfamiliar language he will, by working with a native informant, try to determine the significant generalizations in the grammar of that language. The native informant can, for example, tell him whether or not particular utterances are the same or different utterances syntactically, semantically, or phonologically. There are, however, universal aspects of language, and the linguist will search for the ways in which these aspects are realized in particular languages.

When the linguist has finished writing the grammar of a language he will have, presumably, described all the syntactic, semantic, and phonological information that the native speaker has available to him. There is, obviously, some information that is available to some language users in the linguistic community that is not available to others. For example, there are dialect variations and lexicon variations. However, a large body of information is shared by all members of the community and this sharing makes communication possible. It is this large body of information that the linguist attempts to describe. One of the goals of a description of language acquisition and development is to describe the linguistic information available to the child for use in generating utterances at various stages of development.

Psychologists, on the other hand, are concerned with the ways in which the human organism acquires and uses this competence or knowledge of the language to understand and produce utterances. Granting that the linguistic descriptions can adequately describe this competence, it is still the task of the psychologist to describe performance or the use of this knowledge.

The psychologist tries to account for the fact that the members of the linguistic communities acquire this body of shared information, and he tries to determine the rules for the use of this knowledge. Various learning theories have been proposed to account for the acquisition and use of linguistic competence. These theories have been based, in part, on observations that have been made about the utterances of the child and adult, but, primarily, on extrapolations from experiments which may or may not have been concerned with language per se. In addition, attempts have been made to determine the characteristics of the mechanisms which underly the acquisition and use of language, such as perception, discrimination, memory, and hypotheses formation. These mechanisms are linked, in some manner, to the structures and functions of the nervous system. As Brain stated, ". . . the nature of speech must be considered both psychologically and physiologically."[1] Therefore, attempts have been made to establish the links between psychological mechanisms and the structures and functions of the nervous system. Another goal of a description of language acquisition and development, then, is to describe the processes by which the child acquires language and the psychological mechanisms which underly these processes.

Since, in experimentation, the greatest gains are made when the subjects' external or internal environment can be measurably altered, and, since the subjects of experiments to acquire knowledge about the organization and functioning of the nervous system in performing linguistic tasks should be man, the task of furthering our understanding of the physiology of language is a difficult one. We cannot arbitrarily change man's environment or tamper with his nervous system. The models of the nervous system that have been proposed to account for linguistic performance have been based on the so-called experiments of nature and observation and measurement, wherever possible, of the linguistic behavioral results of these experiments. These experiments are of two kinds: the deviant organism and the developing organism. Theoretical descriptions of the structural and physiological differences which may lead to differences in the linguistic behavior of both children and adults have been presented. A final goal of a description of language acquisition and development is to describe the physiological functions which are the foundations of this behavior.

All of the aspects of studying the process of language acquisition and development, linguistic, psychological, and neurophysiological, are logically interdependent. Despite the fact that research has just begun to allow us to determine the characteristics of language, psychological mechanisms and the functions of the nervous system, there have been indications that both psychological mechanisms and the functions of the nervous system 'behave' selectively in terms of the characteristics of the input to the system. Taking as an example the nature and role of memory in comprehending and generating linguistic structures, the following types of experiments have been carried out.

At the phonological level of the grammar, some evidence to substantiate the theory that both vowels and consonants are coded in short-term memory as a set of distinctive features rather than as a single speech sound has been found.[2] Each of the distinctive features are forgotten semi-independently when subjects are asked to recall these speech sounds. At the syntactic level of the grammar some evidence has been found to suggest that more 'storage space' is required for certain types of sentences than for others regardless of their length.[3] When subjects are asked to recall a sentence and a string of unrelated words, fewer unrelated words are recalled in passive, negative, emphatic, and WH-Question sentences than in active-declarative sentences. Fewer still are recalled in negative-passive or passive-question sentences.

There is also evidence to indicate that children's recall of sentences is dependent on the structure of the sentence and their grammatical competence rather than the length of the sentence. As they mature, and as their grammatical competence changes their recall of sentences changes.[4]

Studies of individuals with left- and right-sided lesions of the auditory cortex indicate the specialization of the auditory area of each hemisphere for processing speech or nonspeech stimuli.[5] There is evidence that, depending on the location of a lesion, aphasic subjects have difficulty in distinguishing or producing speech sounds by confusing certain distinctive features but not others. (For example, p for b, or b for d but not p for s).[6] Depending on the location of a lesion, aphasic subjects may have difficulty in identifying or naming objects by confusing related names (for example, ash tray for cigarette) or difficulty in comprehending or producing syntactic relationships.[7] In summary, there are indications that in some instances aphasic patients have difficulty with either phonological, syntactic, or semantic rules depending on the site of the lesion.

There is also some evidence that children who are labeled as having language and/or articulation disabilities but who do not have any detectable physiological impairment, recall sentences and phonological sequences in a different manner than normal-speaking children. Although these children's responses in the recall situation are different from those of normal-speaking children, they are not different within the group.[8]

There is, therefore, some evidence that the nervous system functions differentially in response to speech versus nonspeech and to the various aspects of the structure of the linguistic message. There is some evidence to indicate that the linguistic message is recalled in terms of the structures that have been described by linguists. The evidence at this time is gross and fleeting. However, there are indications that research which pursues the question of the relationships between the structures of the language and behavior in various experimental conditions will lead to a better understanding of both the psychological mechanisms (such as recall) and physiological functions (such as the nature and structure of memory) which underly this behavior.

The hoped for outcome of the study of language acquisition and development is a description of the linguistic behavior of the child at various stages of development or a description of his changing linguistic competence in terms of (1) the characteristics of the system that is being acquired (the content of his grammar), (2) the characteristics of the psychological mechanisms which underly this changing competence, and (3) the characteristics of the functions of the nervous system which are linked to these underlying mechanisms. Therefore, the techniques and knowledge of all of the disciplines that have concerned themselves with studying the structure of language and its use must be involved in obtaining an understanding of the processes of language acquisition and development.

Various strategies can and have been employed to approach this goal. The effectiveness of these varying strategies should be examined to determine, at present, the best way to proceed in attempting to achieve the hoped for outcome.

1.2 Experimental Approaches to the Study

In studying the perception and production of language by children, we would like to know, first, what are the correlations between the parameters of the physical events (the language in the environment) and the child's discrimination of them. Second, we would like to know the developmental course in these correlations. Third, we would like to know how these discriminations are realized in actual performance. We would like to know what the child knows about language at various stages of development and how he uses this knowledge. Implicit in all these questions is the basic assumption that the parameters of the physical events that are used to understand and produce language are known. We would then know what dimensions to vary experimentally to obtain some measures of change over the developmental course. This, however, is not the case. There are, however, some presuppositions that have been made on both theoretical and experimental grounds.

From some linguistic points of view the parameters important to the use of language cannot be found in the physical events occurring in the environment since these parameters are abstract rules of the syntactic, phonological, and semantic aspects of the language. In large part the argument has been as follows. The structure of the grammar of any language is "abstract" in nature. The physical signal is an obscure representation of the underlying structure of an utterance. To understand the utterance the listener must have knowledge of this underlying structure. Since this knowledge cannot be derived from the physical signal per se, it must be presumed that the child has the capacity to detect and recognize "abstract" features in the signal. The child, therefore, must have the innate capacity to search for the abstract syntactic, phonological, and semantic rules from which sentences are generated.[9] The structures and functions of the nervous system necessary to the acquisition of language are present at birth in the intact organism. The only observable environmental contribution necessary to the acquisition process is that language be present. The process is inevitable and ordered, and its form is determined by the maturation of the nervous system at various stages of development.[10]

From some psychological points of view the parameters of the physical events used to understand and produce sentences are the stimulus-response-reward conditions or the internally elaborated stimulus-response-reward conditions that operate during the acquisition of larger and larger segments of the sentence, or longer and longer sentences, or differing types of sentences. From other psychological points of view the child's general capacity to conceptualize about and perform logical operations with the stimuli in his environment might determine the form of his linguistic behavior during various stages of development.

The important question is how does one go about determining the validity of any of these assumptions.

Outside of the evidence already cited which indicates that the recall of utterances can be dependent on their underlying structure, rather than evident characteristics such as length, there is also evidence to indicate that the acoustic signal is perceived in a manner that has very little to do with the physical parameters of the signal, but, rather, is dependent on the underlying structure of the signal.[11]

We have, however, little data available to us about the development of the nervous system in relation to linguistic performance. At this point very little is known about what the brain does when 'it' understands and produces language. Research from this point of view has been primarily observational; observation of certain maturational changes in the nervous system and observation of presumably concurrent gross changes in linguistic behavioral manifestations such as development from babbling to first word to sentence generation. In addition, there has been a limited amount of observation of what has been termed critical stages of learning. These observations indicate (1) that there may be optimal times during the physiological maturation period for acquiring certain aspects of language, and (2) that the structure and functions of the nervous system are plastic in certain differing ways until the age of puberty so that the child can, presumably, develop unique structural mechanisms for dealing with linguistic data if he is deprived of the 'usual ones' before the age when these functional patterns have solidified.[12]

We have yet to establish definitively the anatomical and physiological bases of the language process, or to describe definitively maturational changes in the nervous system. We have, also, yet to describe definitively the changing structure of the child's use of language over time. It is difficult to attempt to correlate the largely unknown with the largely unknown and derive some explanation of behavior. However, we can pursue this question by describing in detail, rather than grossly, the structure of the utterances used by children during the physiological maturational period critical in the language acquisition process (presumably from birth to puberty) and the structure of the utterances presented to the child in the primary linguistic data during this period. We may, thus, determine the effect of the environmental linguistic conditions on the linguistic performance of the child. The task of establishing and describing the structure and functions of the nervous system in language processing and the changes that occur over the maturational period must obviously be pursued as well. This task can, perhaps, be approached by a detailed description of the utterances used by children with known physiological impairment, as compared to those of children who are physiologically intact.

Psychologists stress the language learning situation or the environmental conditions necessary to the acquisition of language. Most stimulus-response-reward theories suggest that we speak because to speak reduces a drive. The reduction of this drive rewards us for speaking and then speaking becomes functionally autonomous. Undesirable responses are not reinforced and, therefore, become extinguished.[13] Imitation is, in some theories, considered to be a drive. Children, therefore, imitate the behavior of persons in their environment (primarily the mother), and one of these behaviors is verbal.[14] A mediation theory of learning suggests that first associations appear through simple stimulus-response laws (that is, single words). When utterances increase in length the simple S-R laws can no longer account for what is produced and understood. Presumably, at this stage the class formation process begins. That is, for example, by observing that A-B-C and A-B-D occur, the child learns that C and D are members of the same class.[15] Research has shown that in specific situations human subjects can be conditioned to emit certain types of verbal and nonverbal responses, and there have been many experiments in paired-associate learning of word lists. There are two problems associated with approaching the study of the parameters of the stimulus-discrimination correlations occurring in language acquisition and development from this point of view, and they are both concerned with fact. Since these theories in large measure (in the past at least) presuppose that no matter what is being learned the same principles of learning conditions hold, and that the important parameters are variations in the learning conditions, they have precluded the necessity of experimentally varying and analyzing the aspects of the language that are presented or acquired in the learning experience. Therefore, since this aspect of the experimental situation has not been systematically studied, it is useless to suppose that because in laboratory experiments subjects are conditionable and can associate, that either one of these learning conditions is necessary to the acquisition of language. This is especially the case when experimental results can be interpreted in widely different manners.[16]

Some of the techniques that have been developed in the learning laboratory can be used to determine the facts of the changing linguistic competence of the child when the *structure* of the stimulus materials presented in learning situations is recorded, controlled, and systematically varied. These techniques would be especially useful in determining the distinctions in the speech signal that the infant is capable of observing (speech sound differences, stress differences, and intonation differences) during the babbling period until the sentence generation period. With this age group precise and clear determination of response to varying auditory signals is difficult to obtain. Various physiological measures have been used to attempt to determine attention, and possibly differentiation of visual and auditory stimuli such as cardiac rate change[17] and evoked potential response.[18] With the latter technique valid results have been obtained with children 4 years and older. Its usefulness with a younger population is questionable. Many questions remain about the usefulness of either technique in determining stimulus differentiation of a subtle nature by the infant.[19] Use of conditioning techniques may bring forth clearer and more detailed results. The fact that the infant is conditionable under certain stimulus conditions (for example, he will turn his head to find a nipple or see a face in the presence of an auditory signal)[20] provides us with a tool which may be useful in providing information about the child's speech-sound discrimination.

Another approach might be to explore the relationships of cognitive development and language development to see if one can determine cognitive precursors to certain kinds of linguistic performance. Indeed, a long standing argument has developed as to whether cognitive development is dependent on language development, or whether language development is dependent on cognitive development, or whether the two processes are independent. Since both the processes of cognitive development and language development are far from being understood it is difficult to see how any of the positions in the argument can be maintained. For research purposes one can only analyze both processes to determine which aspects of these processes are similar or interdependant. The problem can be approached by developing hypotheses about the organization or structure of both the child's linguistic and non-linguistic conceptualizations by observing how the child actually behaves at various stages of development. These hypotheses can then be tested in various experimental situations. This approach has not been used to describe language acquisition and development. The changing structure of the language that the child uses as he matures has not been described. Therefore, it is difficult to formulate hypotheses to be tested.

Regardless of the theoretical point of view, we find that the basic facts, that is, the structure of what children say and understand at various stages of development, have not been described. Certain observations have been made about the language production of the child over time. It has been observed that the child produces utterances of increasing length and complexity per sampled time as he matures. There has not been, however, a structural description of the process that has been intuitively labeled 'increasing complexity.' We have very little idea from the analyses of the data collected of what actually occurs in this process of increasing complexity, only that it occurs. We have not as yet systematically put the following questions: What is the structure of the set of utterances produced and understood at certain ages? And what are the changes we observe during the course of development in the structure of the set of utterances produced and understood in terms of both content and order? A rather outstanding problem is how to put these questions to the child.

1.3 Structural Descriptions of Utterances

The infant and the very young child cannot simply be treated as a native informant. There is the obvious problem of the difficulty of communicating what is wanted in understandable terms. There is also the problem that the observer is fully competent in the grammar of the language and may find it difficult to maintain the objectivity he is able to maintain when dealing with an unfamiliar language. As any native speaker, he may 'hear' or interpret as being there what is not there simply because he knows what should be there. It is possible that the structural parameters the child is searching for to enable him to understand and produce utterances could be different from those the adult uses and his method of determining those parameters could be very different. In essence, concealing rather than revealing questions may be put by the fully competent speaker-listener to the not fully competent speaker-listener and the interpretation of responses may be biased.

The first order of business would then seem to be to describe structurally the utterances children produce at various stages of development. One can then observe what parameters of the structure of the language the child seems capable of using to generate utterances. The relationship of the structures produced and those understood can then be examined by pertinent experimental questions. For example, we observe that at some stage of development children never produce question sentences that involve auxiliary inversion. They say such things as 'What your name is?' or 'He's sick?' but not 'What is your name?' and 'Is he sick?' What happens when you ask the child to reproduce both the grammatical and nongrammatical utterances? Will he transform the grammatical to the form he produces and repeat the nongrammatical, or will the inverse happen? The answer to this question will give us some evidence about how the structure is understood. Even more importantly the description of the structure of children's utterances will let us know what questions to ask at what time.

We can also begin to ask questions about the relationship between the child's capacity to perform certain cognitive operations and his capacity to perform certain linguistic operations. There are, for example, certain cognitive operations which the child incorporates into his thinking as he matures which will allow him to organize and stabilize his perceptual world. They have been termed 'reversible operations.'[21] There are different linguistic operations which have been termed 'transformations' which can be applied to sentence strings. Knowledge of the operations which can be applied to strings allows the child to observe that, although in some instances the surface structures of strings are different, their underlying meaning is the same (sentence paraphrases) and that although, in other instances, the surface structures of strings may be the same, their underlying meaning is different (ambiguous sentences). Acquisition of this kind of knowledge allows the child to organize and stabilize his linguistic world. We can ask questions about possible relationships between the processes of language development and cognitive development when we have described the operations children use in the utterances they produce and understand. Further, we can begin to observe the sequence of development of these two sets of capacities and observe sequential dependencies if any exist.

The nature of the relationships between the linguistic input and the psychological mechanisms such as memory, perception, and psycho-motor skills which underly the structural changes in the linguistic behavior of the child at various stages of development can be explored when one has determined the structural aspects of the language it would be interesting and reasonable to ask questions about, and at what age. Cues as to what are possibly interesting questions can be obtained from a structural description of the sentences children produce. As an example, questions concerning the changes in the structure of memory for language which take place over the maturational period can be put. The results of the two studies previously cited, which examined the adult's recall of linguistic sequences, indicated that the structure of the sequence affected both the manner of storage for recall (phonological sequences) and the amount of storage space required for recall (syntactic sequences). The following types of questions can be put: Is it the length of the derivational history of a sentence which affects recall? Is it the types of operations involved in the derivation which affect recall? Is it aspects of the sentence which are found in its surface structure which affect recall? Do changes in behavior occur because of increasing memory space or changes in memory organization, and when, during the developmental course, do either of these factors have the greater effect on behavior?

The answers to these questions cannot be obtained by putting them to adults and then applying what has been found to the child. For example, it has been found that adults have no greater difficulty in recalling sentences in which there has been a complex expansion of the auxiliary node than ones in which there has been a simple expansion.[22] Sentences which contain complex expansions of the auxiliary node are produced much later in the developmental sequence than ones with simple expansions,[23] and children have much greater difficulty in reproducing the complex expanded form of the auxiliary than the simple form.[24] One cannot simply assume that the child is 'like' the adult in linguistic performance except for some input and output restrictions of a peripheral or trivial nature.[25] One cannot also simply assume that the child is agrammatical or that his grammar is different from the adult's simply because he is a child and appears to produce utterances that are different from those of the adult.[26] These assumptions must be tested by a careful analysis of what is indeed understood and produced throughout the developmental course.

Finally we wish to understand the nature of the physiological functions, psychological mechanisms, and environmental variables which make for 'differences' in the linguistic performance of children at various stages of development.

A great majority of the children in any linguistic environment acquire and develop language normally. That is, the great majority of children communicate adequately enough in their linguistic community so that their language comprehension and production is not marked as being different by other members of the community. There are some children, however, whose language deviates so strikingly from the linguistic models of both their peers and their elders that communication becomes difficult or impossible. An important and nontrivial distinction to be made between normal and non-normal speakers, then, is how adequately the child is communicating with other members of his linguistic community. In this way we eliminate from this particular discussion style variations and dialect variations.

We may find, for example, that for a given period of sampled time a child produces a significantly higher percentage of negative, or imperative, or question sentences than his peers. We may find that for a given period of sampled time a child produces a significantly higher percentage of sentences which contain If-Then Clauses or Because Clauses than do his peers. We may discover something important and interesting about his personality or his way of thinking about problems. However, we will have discovered nothing about the differences in the capacity of children to perform linguistic operations.

We may also find, for example, that, in a given linguistic community, pluralization and tense are realized in a somewhat different manner by the children in that community than in another linguistic community although the 'native' language is presumably the same. However, we also find that all members of this community are marking pluralization and tense in the same manner. It is difficult to see how this performance can be marked deficient or abnormal. When the functional relationships, classes, and phonological re-lationships, possibly the linguistic universals, found in the language used by the child's linguistic community are not found in the child's language at a certain stage of development, his language acquisition and development can be marked as being different.[27] What is implied in this statement is that it is necessary to describe the sentences children use within a given linguistic community over the developmental course before judgements of 'difference' can be made. The differences between linguistic communities in the structure of the language used which break down communication between communities and the effect this has on the development of the children is an important question. However, it should not be confused with attempting to determine the nature of the physiological function differences, or psycho-logical mechanisms differences, or environmental differences which make for differences in the linguistic capacity and performance of children within a community.

We may isolate populations of children whose linguistic behavior, that is the structure of the sentences they use, indicates that the processes of language acquisition and development are different for them than for the other children in their linguistic community. Their linguistic behavior may deviate from the norm in different ways. They may deviate in the phono-logical, syntactic, or semantic structures they use, or in any combination of these aspects. We may then attempt to determine the factors which have contributed to these differences.

It has been stated that the course of language development is shaped primarily by the development of the child's nervous system together with his innate capacity to search for and discover abstract features in the physical signal. It has also been stated that the course of language development is shaped primarily by the environmental learning conditions and the child's 'capacity to learn.'[28] Some of the physiological factors which may contribute to differences *of a certain kind* are evident. We can determine whether or not the child has a hearing loss, has a visual loss, has paralysis of parts of the vocal mechanism and, in some instances, whether the child is brain-damaged. However, in some instances the child may have a language disorder and there is no gross evidence of physiological damage. The disorder may be accounted for by a physiological impairment we cannot measure or by an environmental deprivation we cannot determine, or possibly both.

Structural descriptions of the language used by these children (both those evidently physiologically impaired and those with whom physiological dam-age is not obvious) can define in a detailed manner the ways in which their linguistic behavior deviates from the norm. We can determine the way in which these children understand and produce the syntactic, semantic, and phonological relationships and properties of the language as compared to normal populations at various ages. Experimentation, examining the performance of these children in linguistic tasks, may isolate differences in the structure of the psychological mechanisms such as perception, memory, and hypotheses formation underlying the performance of these tasks. We may even be able to determine differences in the physiological structures and functions which are not easily observable, as we become more sophisticated about the operation of the nervous system. We may thus isolate the mechanisms necessary and critical to normal acquisition when we systematically compare the linguistic performance of normal and deviant populations.

The answer to the question of the varying contribution of physiological and environmental factors seems to be a difficult one to obtain with a deviant population. It is difficult to determine whether the linguistic behavior of the deaf, blind, or brain-damaged child should primarily be accounted for by the fact of his physiological impairment or the reaction of his environment to his impairment. Even the application of a diagnostic label such as deaf, aphasic, mentally retarded, etc., does not guarantee that we have isolated the factors which have determined a child's linguistic behavior. It has been found that factors such as age of onset of impairment, and, presumably such factors as intelligence, emotional stability of the child, and educational experience can contribute to shaping a child's linguistic behavior in these instances. Matters are even further complicated by the evidence that sensory deprivation can bring about physiological changes in the organism over time.[29] The situation becomes even more confused in the many instances in which damage to the nervous system is suspected but there is no hard evidence of this (that is, the so-called minimally brain-damaged child). In essence these children probably present unique instances of the interaction of physiological and environmental factors.

The answer to the question can best be obtained with children who are acquiring language normally and by observation of the actual environmental conditions which occur and manipulations of these conditions. Environmental conditions have been manipulated and changes in performance have occurred. For example, gross output has been shown to increase when there is increased stimulation of a certain kind.[30] It has been found that family occupation (that is business, clerical, and professional versus laboring) significantly affects the variety of sounds produced and the frequency with which sounds are produced from about 1 1/2 to 2 1/2 years of age. Before 1 1/2 years, age is the only significant factor affecting type and frequency.[31] This evidence, however, does not indicate that experimental manipulation of environmental conditions can alter the course of language development.

Despite the fact that some subjects did not receive increased stimulation they nevertheless acquired the speech sound system of their language. Both children who were in laboring families as well as those in nonlaboring families acquired the speech-sound system of their language. Evidence of structural differences must be found.

Throughout this discussion the importance of obtaining structural descriptions of the sentences children use has been stressed. However, the fact that this is only a first step in obtaining an explanation of the processes of language acquisition and development is evident. We are not only interested in the linguistic description of what the child may be producing and understanding, but also in determining the psychological mechanisms and physiological functions which underly his performance. This does not mean descriptions of style and dialect variations, although this is an aspect of language development which has yet to be explored and could also profit from systematic structural description. We wish to find the generalizations that can be observed from child to child and the relationship of these generalizations to what is known or hypothesized about the use of mechanisms in the child's development in perceiving, abstracting, storing, and problem solving. It is through a structural description of the utterances the child uses and an experimental exploration and description of the mechanisms the child uses to understand and produce these utterances that we hope to find these relationships. Structural descriptions of utterances provide information about the linguistic parameters that should make up the content of experiments at various stages of development.

1.4 Limitations of Structural Descriptions

There should be limitations imposed on the interpretation of structural descriptions. In some instances interpretations may be premature, and the gathering of data over a sufficient period of developmental time will reveal that errors of interpretation have been made. In other instances the situation is not so clear. The structural description of an utterance may be perfectly evident, and there is no question of descriptive error. However, the interpretation of the description is very much open to experimenter bias.

One of the problems in attempting to describe and interpret the descriptions of the utterances children produce is obtaining a complete picture of a particular grammatical development. We must observe what is happening over a large enough period of developmental time. For example, it has been observed that at some stage of development the child is producing utterances which contain the contracted form of the Copula ('I'm,' 'he's,' etc.).[32] What is also observed is that there are no instances of utterances in which the copula appears without the Pronoun such as 'mommy's here.'

Also the child produces utterances such as 'he good' and 'he's good' with about equal frequency. At some later stage of development the copula is used with Noun Subjects, although alternations such as 'mommy here' and 'mommy's here' still occur. At the earlier stage the Copula might be described as being independent of the Pronoun since it is being produced. However, data from the later stage which reveals the contrast of contexts in which it is used (with Nouns as well as Pronouns) indicates that to describe the Copula as independent at the earlier stage would be a descriptive error. It has also been found that children produce the past form of irregular Verbs (for example, 'came') before they produce the past form of regular Verbs.[33] The utterances containing this past form could be described as containing the structure Verb + past. However, the fact that at some later stage of development one observes the regular past being attached to the irregular Verb (comed) as well as being attached to regular Verbs (walked), and the fact that the correct past form of the strong Verb reappears at an even later stage (came) indicates that the description Verb + past of the early 'came' is a descriptive error. In the development of any type of syntactic relationship or restrictive rule, piecemeal observations can lead to descriptive errors.

There are also problems of interpretations of descriptions in which descriptive error is not involved. For example, it has been observed that the early forms of negation can be described as additions of a negative element to a sentence (for example, 'no wipe finger').[34] This has been interpreted as being nontransformational in nature.[35] It has also been observed that the imperative form appears early in the sequence of development (for example, 'go up'). This form has been interpreted as being transformational in nature since it must involve the deletion of 'you.'[36] It is possible to interpret early negation as a transformation if one holds the position that addition of an element is a transformational operation. It is possible to interpret early imperative utterances as nontransformational if one observes the possibility that early utterances often do not contain any Pronoun element (for example, 'want dollie'). The fact that early negatives are not like adult forms and early imperatives are, would not be assumed by an experimenter to imply that one is transformational in structure and the other is not.

At some later stage of development it has been observed that many children produce utterances which contain Relative Clauses of the following type:

1. I've got the book you want.

2. I saw the lady who was here yesterday.

However, even at age 7, children much more rarely produce utterances such as:

3. The book that you want is on the table.

4. The lady who was here yesterday came back.

All these utterances might, and have been labeled as containing a single clause and lumped together as a type of utterance. Although utterances 1 through 4 are all derived from two underlying sentences and all involve embedding, the operation of embedding S2 within S1 is a later productive acquisition than embedding at the end of S1. The observation that preschool children produce sentences which contain clauses is correct and the observation that children do generate sentences which involve the operation of embedding is also correct. The interpretation that children during the preschool period have acquired the competence to embed would be inaccurate. They have acquired the competence to perform a certain kind of embedding but not all kinds. To overlook this fact would obscure an important developmental trend and, perhaps, some important information about what makes certain types of structures easier to understand and produce than others. This, in turn, might be related to the child's capacity to perform certain cognitive operations before others.

The severest limitation on the interpretation of structural descriptions of the sentences that children produce is that we cannot be sure that they completely reveal what children understand about sentences. Although they do not produce completely well-formed negatives at some stage, or embeddings within sentences we do not know whether they understand them or not. Inversely, although they are producing sentences of a certain type one cannot be sure that they are being understood in the manner in which they are described. It is possible that there are differences between a child's production grammar and his comprehension grammar. Along with structural descriptions of the sentences children produce, the child's ability to understand sentences of varying structure, both well-formed and not, should be examined. Descriptions of the kinds of structures children both comprehend and produce will not only give us information about the facts of the developmental course in language acquisition but will point the way to insightful questions about the psychological and physiological mechanisms which underly this course. Taking as an example one aspect of syntactic rules, it is possible that production is limited by motoric factors (for example, inability to produce a final sibilant for pluralization), or by comprehension factors (for example, no understanding of the rule for pluralization in the grammar), or by phonological rule factors (no application of rules for pluralization in the grammar). The factors which may be operating at various stages of development may be parceled out by first observing what is occurring in the utterances produced at various stages and then putting to the child what seem to be reasonable and feasible experimental questions. Can the child produce the final sibilants in non-plural contexts, but not with plurals (that is, he produces "nose" but not "trees")? Can he respond correctly but nonverbally to plural, nonplural contrasts? Can he learn rules for pluralization in unique situations (that is, for example 'wafim' and 'wafi' versus 'waf' and 'wafs')? Does the particular phonological context make a difference in performance (that is, 'muffs' versus 'fans' versus 'roses')? Knowing whether the child produces only what he comprehends or comprehends only what he produces is important since this knowledge can lead to a better explanation of the techniques the child uses to acquire a language.

1.5 Some General Comments

In the attempt to describe structurally the utterances children use, several directions can be taken. One can choose to describe the acquisition of a class in the language such as Noun, Verb, or Determiner and trace its development in all possible contexts. The syntactic and semantic rules observed in the use of the class can be observed over the maturational period. The phonological composition of members of this class can be observed as well. Alternatively one can choose to describe the development of particular types of sentences such as negative sentences, relative clause sentences, or conjunction sentences. Another choice might be to concentrate either on the syntactic or morphological or phonological or semantic structures the child is using during the maturational period. Ideally, one would like to describe the complete grammar of children over the maturational period. Parceling out various aspects of the grammar for description, in all likelihood distorts the picture of grammatical development since all aspects of the grammar are interdependent. This is probably most true of the earliest stage of development when the processes of differentiation and definition seem to be just beginning.

Choosing to describe the syntactic structures being used by children throughout the developmental period seems to be a logical beginning, however, since it has been postulated that it is the derived deep structure of the string which is semantically interpreted[37] and the transformed structure of the string that is phonologically interpreted.[38] It should nevertheless be stressed that incorporated into this semantic theory is a dictionary as well as semantic interpretative rules, and it has been very carefully pointed out in this phonological theory[39] that there is a distinction between morpheme structure rules which apply before transformations and phonological rules which apply after transformations. How the child acquires a dictionary and relates the properties of lexical items to a sequence of phonemic features is obviously of great importance.

Within the syntactic component of the grammar, there are two classes of structures: base structures and transformations. Most of the discussion that follows is concerned with a description of the use of these two classes or rules. In the discussion of the use of base structure rules, however, it will be necessary to comment on semantic and phonological properties and rules.

In an age range of about 3 1/2 to 4 1/2 years all the basic syntactic structures postulated to be used by adults are used by some children. Studies using various kinds of descriptive techniques have found that preschool children use as 'complex' sentence types as those used by adults. McCarthy, for example,[40] found that preschool children were using complex and elaborated sentences. The classification by McCarthy labeled this type of sentence as the most sophisticated type used by adults. Obviously a great deal of language development has occurred by this age period, but a great deal of language development of a different kind is observed to occur after this age period until age 7 (the last age sampled in the research to be reported) and probably beyond this age. This continuing development takes place in several forms: use of elaborated forms of basic structures and use of differing types of transformational operations, observation of selectional restrictions, and elimination of certain approximations to complete sets of rules. We shall attempt in the following pages to describe what is meant by basic structures and what is meant by continuing grammatical development. Emphasis will be placed on the operations involved in the generation of structures used by children rather than a labeling of these structures. We will try to trace the course of this development up to age 7 as evidenced both by the sentences children produce and by the sentences they reproduce. The word 'trace' is appropriate since, at this stage of the research in language development, effort should be expended on determining the facts of developmental trends which can then lead us to pertinent detailed questions.

From about age 2 to 3 children whose utterances have been structurally described are few in number. However, the utterances these children produced and the contexts in which they were produced have been periodically sampled and recorded. Therefore, one could observe the grammatical development of the same child over a critical period of language development. Over 150 children contributed to the results obtained in the age range of just under 3 years to just over 7 years. However, in this age range language was sampled only at one age.

With this latter group speech was elicited and tape recorded in three stimulus situations: responses to a projective test,[41] conversation with an adult (the experimenter) generated by some of the questions suggested in the test manual, and additional questions introduced by the experimenter (every child was given the same questions), and conversation with peers generated by role playing in a game about the family. Therefore, an effort was made to sample language in 'typical' situations.[42]

There were seventy-nine boys and seventy-three girls in the population in which language was sampled. There was no significant difference in measured I.Q. between grade levels (preschool through first grade), or between boys and girls. The I.Q. for all groups was measured by the Full Range Vocabulary Test.[43] Parental occupation for all the children fell within the upper 24 per cent range of a middle class population.[44]

Sex, I.Q., and situation were never significantly correlated with numbers of varying syntactic structures used. Boys did not use significantly more structures than girls or vice versa at different grade levels. Children with I.Q.'s above the mean for their grade level did not use significantly more structures than did the children below the mean I.Q. Differing stimulus situations resulted in differing total outputs (number of sentences) for some children but not the number of varying syntactic structures used. Age was the only significant variable of the variables tested. One might ask why this is so when much of the literature about language development notes sex and I.Q. differences. This difference in results is probably due to the fact that basic syntactic structures were not being described but, rather, measures of language which may be affected by these variables and also experimenter and situation variables. Such measures are mean sentence length, total output, and number or variations of vocabulary items. It would also seem logical to suppose that the rules of a child's grammar would impose the restrictions on the varying types of structures rather than a particular stimulus situation imposing restrictions. The determination of those variables which do significantly affect the acquisition and use of basic syntactic structures is indeed one of the hoped for outcomes of structural descriptions of the sentences children use.

Notes

1. R. Brain, "The neurology of language," *Brain, 84,* 146 (1961).
2. W. A. Wickelgren, "Distinctive features and errors in short-term memory for English vowels," *J. Acoust. Soc. Am., 38,* 583-588 (1965); "Distinctive features and errors in short-term memory for English consonants," *J. Acoust. Soc. Am., 39,* 388-398 (1966).
3. H. B. Savin and E. Perchonock, "Grammatical structure and immediate recall of English sentences," *J. Verbal Learning Verbal Behavior, 4,* 348-353 (1965).

4. This aspect of development is discussed in Chapter 4.
5. D. Kimura, "Cerebral dominance and the perception of verbal stimuli," *Canad. J. Psychol., 15,* 166-171 (1961); D. Shankweiler; "Effects of temporal lobe damage on perception of dichotically presented melodies," *J. Comp. Physiol. Psychol., 62,* 115-119 (1966).
6. A. R. Luria, "Factors and forms of aphasia." In *Disorders of Language,* Ciba Foundation Symposium (Boston: Little,Brown, 1964), pp. 112-167.
7. R. Jakobson, "Towards a linguistic typology of aphasia." In *Disorders of Language,* Ciba Foundation Symposium (Boston: Little, Brown, 1964), pp. 2-42.
8. See Chapter 4.
9. N. Chomsky, *Aspects of the Theory of Syntax* (Cambridge, Mass.: The M.I.T. Press, 1965), Chap. 1.
10. E. Lenneberg, "The natural history of language." In F. Smith and G. A. Miller, eds., *Genesis of Language* (Cambridge, Mass.: The M.I.T. Press, 1966), pp. 219-252.
11. For example, P. Lieberman, "On the acoustic basis of the perception of intonation by linguists," *Word, 21,* 40-53 (1965); J. Fodor and T. Bever, "The psychological reality of linguistic segments," *J. Verbal Learning Verbal Behavior, 4,* 414-420 (1965).
12. E. H. Lenneberg (among others), "Speech development: its anatomical and physiological concomitants." In E. C. Carterette, ed., *Brain Function, Vol. III: Speech, Language and Communication* (Berkeley, Calif.: University of California Press, 1966), pp. 37-66. Lenneberg has noted that, with brain-damaged children, the earlier a lesion is suffered, the better the chance for more normal linguistic performance. This, of course, may be dependent on the site of the lesion. The study of the development of language by those children whose hearing mechanism has been congenitally impaired would give us insights into the capacity of the human organism to acquire and use a communication system when the 'usual' mechanisms · are damaged. The study of the question of critical stages of learning is particularly appropriate with this population since they provide instances in which language has been introduced at varying ages. Most of these children use some form of manual communication even though they may not be communicating vocally. The structure of this form of communication, when it is not simply finger spelling, has become a matter of great interest not only to educators of the deaf but also to those concerned with language development and cognitive development. An example of an attempt to describe the structure of this form of communication is W. C. Stokoe, *Sign Language Structure: An Outline of the Visual Communication Systems of the American Deaf* (Wash., D.C.: Gallaudet College, 1960).
13. J. Dollard and N. E. Miller, *Personality and Psychotherapy* (New York: McGraw-Hill, 1950).
14. O. H. Mowrer, "Hearing and speaking: an analysis of language learning," *J. Speech Hearing Disorders, 23,* 143-153 (1960).
15. J. Jenkins and D. S. Palermo, "Mediation processes and the acquisition of linguistic structure." In U. Bellugi and R. Brown, eds., *The Acquisition of Language* (Lafayette, Ind.: Monographs of the Society for Research in Child Development, No. 29, 1964), pp. 141-169.
16. P. J. Waler and J. C. Marshall, "The organization of linguistic performance." In J. Lyons and R. J. Waler, eds. *Psycholinguistics Papers* (Chicago: Aldine, 1966). The authors offer evidence that the results obtained by associationist experimenters and described by their theories can be explained by the semantic skills and strategies of subjects and that this same competence can characterize results which run counter to associationist theory.
17. J. Kagan and M. Lewis, "Studies of attention in the human infant," *Merrill-Palmer Quarterly, 2,* 95-127 (1965).
18. H. Davis, S. K. Hirsh, J. Shelnutt, and C. Bowers, "Further validation of evoked response audiometry (ERA)," *J. Speech Hearing Research, 10,* 717-732 (1967).

19. There is a great deal of difference between determining whether the child can detect the presence of sound at different intensity levels, or distinguish between the human voice and music and determining whether he can distinguish between speech sound sequences such as "pa" and "ma."

20. L. P. Lipsitt (among others), "Learning in the first year of life." In L. P. Lipsitt and C. C. Spiker, eds., *Advances in Child Development and Behavior* (New York: Academic Press, 1963), pp. 147-196.

21. B. Inhelder and J. Piaget, *The Growth of Logical Thinking from Childhood to Adolescence* (New York: Basic Books, 1958).

22. G. A. Miller and K. McKean, "A chronometric study of some relations between sentences," *Quart. J. of Exptl. Psychol., 16,* 297-308 (1964). The verb forms examined were V+past, (have) V+past, (was) V+progressive, (have) (been) V+progressive.

23. See Chapter 3.

24. See Chapter 4.

25. N. Chomsky, "The general properties of language." In F. L. Darley, ed., *Brain Mechanisms Underlying Speech and Language* (New York: Grune and Stratton, 1967), p. 88. Chomsky has stated ". . . there might be a filtering device or a projection device of some kind that operates on deep structure in some non-normal fashion in the children to give other kinds of signals." What seems to be implied in this statement is that the child 'has' all the deep structure of the language but that perception and production are deformed by some mechanisms which disappear in time. The evidence for there being a dissolution of barriers to fully competent grammatical performance rather than a building of competence during the developmental course is not easily obtainable.

26. W. R. Miller, ("The acquisition of grammatical rules by children," paper presented at Linguistic Society of America Annual Meeting, December 1964) has stated, "Recent research . . . clearly shows that the first multi-word sentences of the child are patterned. Whether such patterns can be considered evidence of grammatical structure is debatable, but I would be inclined to think not." The only logical alternative to viewing these early utterances as evidence of grammatical structure is to consider them memorized items. There is ample evidence that these utterances are not direct imitations of what is said by adult speakers. In the face of an inclination to think that early productions are not evidence of grammatical structure, despite the fact that they are patterned and the fact that they are not imitations of the primary linguistic data, it is difficult to conceive of the kind of evidence that would be convincing.

27. See R. Jakobson, "Implications of language universals for linguistics." In J. H. Greenberg, ed., *Universals of Language* (Cambridge Mass.: The M.I.T. Press, 1963), pp. 208-219, for a discussion of those aspects of language which might be considered linguistic universals. Attempts to describe how universals are realized in different communities may clarify concepts of difference and point the way to more productive procedures of educating children from differing linguistic communities.

28. D. S. Palermo, "On learning to talk." Research Bulletin No. 61, Dept. of Psychology, University Park: Penn. State U., Feb. 1966.

29. D. H. Hubel and T. N. Wiesel, "Receptive fields, binocular interaction and functional architecture in the cat's visual cortex," *J. Physiol., 160,* 106-154 (1962).

30. H. L. Rheingold *et al.,* "Social conditioning of vocalizations in the infant," *J. Comp. Physiol. Psychol., 52* (1959).

31. O. C. Irwin, "Infant speech: the effect of family occupational status and of age on use of sound types," *J. Speech Disorders, 13,* 31-34 (1948); O. C. Irwin, "Infant speech: the effect of family occupational status and of age on sound frequency," *J. Speech Disorders, 13,* 320-323 (1948).

32. J. Gruber, "Topicalization in child language." Mimeo, Cambridge, Mass.: M.I.T. Modern Languages Dept., March 29, 1966.

33. S. Ervin, "Structure in children's language." Paper presented at International Congress of Psychology, Washington, 1963.
34. E. S. Klima and U. Bellugi, "Syntactic regularities in the speech of children." In J. Lyons and R. J. Wales, eds., *Psycholinguistics Papers* (Chicago: Aldine, 1966), pp. 183-208.
35. D. McNeill, "Developmental psycholinguistics." In F. Smith and G. A. Miller, eds., *The Genesis of Language* (Cambridge, Mass.: The M.I.T. Press, 1966), pp. 15-84.
36. The description of early forms of negation, imperative, and question will be discussed in greater detail in Chapter 3. These two forms are simply mentioned here to indicate the possible problems in the interpretation of data.
37. J. J. Katz and J. A. Fodor, "The structure of a semantic theory." In J. A. Fodor and J. J. Katz, eds., *The Structure of Language* (Englewood Cliffs, N.J.: Prentice-Hall, 1964), pp. 479-518.
38. Halle, M. "Questions of linguistics." N. 2 des Supplemento al Vol. *13*, Serie X, del *Nuovo Cimento*, 494-517, 1959.
39. *Ibid.*, pp. 515-516.
40. D. McCarthy, *Language Development of the Pre-school Child* (Minneapolis: University of Minnesota Press, 1930).
41. G. S. Blum, *The Blacky Pictures: A Technique for Exploration of Personality Dynamics*, Manual (New York: Psychological Corp., 1950).
42. A detailed description of the population and data collection is given in P. Menyuk, "Syntactic structures in the language of children," *J. Child Develop.*, *34*, 407-422 (1963).
43. R. B. Ammons and H. S. Ammons, *Full Range Picture Vocabulary* (Missoula, Montana: Psychological Test Specialists, 1958).
44. Institute of Child Welfare, *The Minnesota Scale for Parental Occupation* (Minneapolis: University of Minnesota, 1950).

2 Base Structures in Sentences

The base component of the grammar has been described as consisting of a categorial component which implicitly defines what a sentence is and what the basic grammatical relations in the sentence are. The base component includes a lexical component with subcategorization rules within which are marked contextual constraints. The lexical items in a string are marked by syntactic, semantic, and phonological properties. There are elements in the string which indicate that certain transformations can or must be applied.[1] The functional relationships in the sentence (Subject, Predicate, and Object) are implicit in the base structure string and these functional relationships define classes. In a sentence the Subject is the Noun Phrase of the sentence, the Object is the Noun Phrase of the Verb Phrase, and the Predicate is the Verb Phrase of the sentence. Thus, the classes Noun and Verb are defined by their functions in sentences.

To understand and generate sentences the child must observe the functional relationships in sentences, then define types of classifications, and then observe selectional constraints on the combination of these classes. The selectional constraints are imposed by the semantic and syntactic properties of the lexical items in the string and local combination rules. The following is a limited description of base component structures:

Syntactic classes

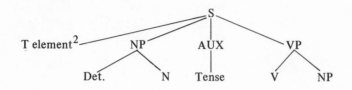

- - - - - - - - - - - - - - - - - - -

Dictionary entries[3]

Syntactic properties

Art.	Human		
Definite	Male	Present	Transitive
	⋮		⋮

Semantic properties

Art.	Human	Present	Transitive
Definite	Male		to perform
	Singular		⋮
	Child		
	⋮		

Phonological features[4]

Logically, the first task of the child would be to determine what a sentence is and what the functional relationships in sentences are, so that he has a basic understanding of the utterances he hears. He can then proceed to defining classes. Hypotheses about what the child knows about language at the earliest stages of development must be highly speculative. Not only have structural descriptions of these utterances been limited to those produced by a small number of children, but the aspects of these utterances which might be most informative about possible underlying structure have not been examined and described.

2.1 Acquisition of the Structure Sentence and Relationships and Classes

Most researchers have begun their analysis of the syntactic structures used by children at the point at which the child is stringing two *recognizable* morphemes together. However, it has been observed that before this period the child is producing sentence-like utterances. Some utterances he produces are single recognizable morphemes. Others are strings of utterances with no recognizable morphemes but marked by stress and differing intonational patterns. The single-morpheme utterances have been called 'sentence-like' and are also presumably marked by stress and differing intonational patterns.[5] These are simply observations, and no careful analysis of the stress and intonational patterns of these early utterances has been undertaken. These single-morpheme utterances might be described as having the following underlying structure:

1. X $\longrightarrow$ phonetic sequence
2. X $\longrightarrow$ phonetic sequence and semantic property/s
3. S $\longrightarrow$ phonetic sequence and semantic property/s
4. X $\longrightarrow$ phonological features and semantic property/s
5. S $\longrightarrow$ phonological features and semantic property/s

The first description of underlying structure which implies that these are completely random utterances must be rejected on the grounds that these sequences are not produced randomly. Although the child may not be producing an 'exact' replication of the adult version, a given phonetic sequence is presumably consistently used by the child in asking for, pointing to, or getting an action or object, and is recognized by the adult as referring to this action or object. Therefore, the second description seems to be the more accurate one. However, descriptions 3 through 5 might also be appropriate at this stage of development. These single morphemes might or might not be considered sentences. The phonetic sequences produced might be derived from underlying phonological features that the child has distinguished in the linguistic data or simply be memorized productions.

The answer to these questions lies in an analysis of the prosodic features of these utterances. Lieberman[6] has noted that the scope of a breath group in several languages can encompass the constituent *sentence*. At the end of an "unmarked" breath group there is a falling fundamental frequency contour. The end of a "marked" breath group has a terminal not-falling fundamental frequency contour. In several languages interrogative sentences which contain a question morpheme can be produced on a normal breath group and the fundamental frequency falls at the end of the sentence. In these same languages (Japanese and English, for example) sentences without a question morpheme all conclude with a rising intonation. Emphasis (or contrastive stress) can be indicated by a momentary increase in the subglottal air pressure on the appropriate part of the breath group and a rise in fundamental frequency. In the case of single morpheme utterances contrastive stress would be indicated by placing this increase in subglottal air pressure on the single morpheme.

If these single morpheme utterances are prosodically marked, they can be interpreted as emphatic statements (!), questions (?), or declaratives (.). If this is the case then these productions have sentence status and it can be postulated that the child at this stage has determined the structure 'sentence.' At a later stage of development, utterances such as 'that there' may be interpreted as '(put) that there!' or '(is) that there?' or 'that (is) there.,' depending on both the context in which the utterance was produced and the intonational pattern and stress of the utterance.

First sentences may have the following underlying structure:

$$S \longrightarrow \text{Topic} + \text{Intonational marker}^7$$

$$\text{Topic} \longrightarrow \left\{ \begin{array}{l} \text{phonetic} \\ \text{phonological} \end{array} \right\} \text{ string}$$

$$\text{Intonational marker} \longrightarrow (.) \quad (!) \quad (?)$$

However, we might also postulate that these intonational markers are learned only in association with particular sound sequences and that the sound sequence plus the intonational marker are memorized items. The child may produce certain items in his lexicon with the question marker, others with the declarative marker, and still others with the emphatic marker and never produce utterances in which markers are exchanged. In that case the structure of the utterances would be

$$S \longrightarrow \text{Topic}$$

$$\text{Topic} \longrightarrow \left\{ \begin{array}{l} \text{phonetic} \\ \text{phonological} \end{array} \right\} \text{ string} + \text{Intonational marker}$$

It is an extremely pertinent question to determine whether or not the child uses intonational markers generatively. The answer to this question will tell us how the child may possibly store in memory and use syntactic structures at an early stage of development. The answer can be derived from analyses of the prosodic features of these utterances. The phonetic features in the early productions must also be analyzed to obtain a more accurate description of underlying structure. It has been observed that single word utterances are marked prosodically. There is evidence that the child differentiates between unmarked and marked utterances.[8] However, the evidence that these features have been isolated from particular forms has not been obtained.

The structure of the term 'topic' in the description of these single morpheme utterances must be examined. A very random sampling of the utterances produced by two children at this stage of development indicates that Nouns, Verbs, Adjectives, and Prepositions, according to traditional classification appear. The assumption that all single-morpheme utterances are Nouns is not borne out in this very limited sample of children. The following is a list of examples of the morphemes used by these children:[9]

Noun	Verb	Adjective	Preposition
light	go	nice	up
bottle	look	good	down
car	sit	pretty	on

The term 'topic' used in the description of these strings does not, then, imply that all morphemes produced at this stage are Nouns. Dichotomization of the above productions into traditional linguistic classes would seem to be incorrect. There is no evidence that they are being functionally used in the same manner as defined by labels (that is, Adjective, Noun, Verb, etc.). The utterance may be the name of an object (car), action (look), state (good), direction (up), but they also may presumably take a declarative form ((that's a) car.), an imperative form (look (at x)!) and ((pick me) up!) or a question form ((am I) nice?). Therefore, these utterances do not seem to be entered in the child's dictionary as separate syntactic classes with distinct semantic properties. As was stated, we have no information about how freely the prosodic features are used with the items in the child's lexicon at this stage of development, but only the information that they are used.

It has been observed that not all children go through a single morpheme utterance stage or, if they do, it is very fleeting. This observation may be the result of whether or not single morphemes are recognized by the adults who are listening to the child's utterances or it may, indeed, be the case that some children proceed immediately to two or three morpheme utterances after the so-called 'babbling' period. Their performance may be analogous to those of children who walk without going through the crawling stage. However, before any child walks he must first be able to turn over, sit up, and stand up. Specific competences precede his ability to move from a prone to a standing position and from this position to walking. It seems highly unlikely that there are not specific linguistic generalizations that the child has made and specific competences he has achieved before he proceeds to produce two and three morpheme-length utterances. Presumably there should be links between what the child understands and produces at this early stage of development and what he understands and produces at a somewhat later stage. The first syntactic acquisition, therefore, may be a demarcation of the structure 'sentence.'

Structural descriptions of the utterances children produce and of the aspects of the sentences they are able to discriminate during the period labeled 'babbling' until the period labeled 'sentence production' have not, as yet, been undertaken. One might look at single morpheme utterances from two widely different points of view: they are stored in memory as a sequence of sounds which are inseparable and these sequences are verbal symbols of auditory, visual, or tactile images; *or* they are stored in memory as the syntactic structure sentence with semantic properties and phonological features to which intonational markers, also stored in memory, are applied as these sequences are generated. The latter, and stronger claim might be made for several reasons. There is some evidence that intonational markers are applied and that these utterances are interpreted as sentences in some instances. There is some evidence that children differentiate between prosodically marked and unmarked utterances. Finally, there is some evidence that children from two very different linguistic environments master, first, speech sounds which are composed of certain phonological features as compared to those speech sounds which do not contain these features.[10] The particular morphemes that a child uses first and continues to use are the result of the child's exposure to particular environmental situations. It is obvious, for example, that the morpheme 'car' would not appear early in the lexicon of a child born in an environment in which cars do not exist. However, observation of the child's translation of the structure of morphemes in the primary linguistic data into unique phonetic utterances will give us some evidence as to whether or not phonological features are distinguished at this stage. Of course, if the underlying structure of utterances produced at this stage can be described as the constituent 'sentence,' and if prosodic features are applied generatively, and if phonological distinctions are being made, what is observed in the utterances produced very shortly thereafter is more easily explained. The corroboration of this strong position lies in an analysis of the use of prosodic features and the use of distinctive phonological features by children during this stage of development. Assuming this strong position forces us to ask these questions, whereas assuming the weaker position, that these utterances are simply memorized verbal labels for an object in the environment allows us to ignore them.

In addition to this, several critical questions remain unanswered. First, we do not know what role the babbling period plays in the development of 'real' language. Further, until the child begins to produce utterances which are accepted by the adults in his environment as morphemes, he is said to be babbling. The reason for the decision on the part of the adult that the child is producing meaningful sequences at some stage and not another is often unclear. Therefore, second, we do not in fact know when the child ceases to babble and produces 'real' language. An understanding of the process of mapping sound components into meaningful utterances cannot be obtained until the transition has been defined and the parameters of this transition are understood.

Children proceed from single-morpheme utterances to utterances which contain two or more morphemes. Why children do this might be, and has been, explained as the necessity of conveying more specific meaning in an expanding world (a world which now may include peers as well as parents) in some economical manner. One can get more than one block, for example, by stating 'block' and then 'more.' It is more economical to state 'more block.' At some later stage, one might assume, that it will be necessary to convey the meaning of 'want all (or) red (or) lots (or) some blocks.' The need to convey more specific meaning in an economical manner can be applied as a general explanation for any developmental change that is observed in the child's linguistic performance. However, to state that this is the reason for the developmental change ignores the important fact that the child does not immediately proceed to more precise definition and, for example, by the use of Quantifiers and Adjectives in his utterances, such as those mentioned above, achieve even more definition with even greater economy. It might be hypothesized that the child's memory or output mechanism is restricted to producing only two- or three-morpheme-length utterances. If this is so, the particular content of these utterances must be explained. They are rarely replications of first or last things heard. It might also be hypothesized that at this stage the child has the competence to express some functional relationships in sentences and that this is the present limit of his syntactic competence. If we postulate that it is through his understanding of these relationships that he will eventually be able to define the classes in his language, this seems to be a logical hypothesis.

Just as in the case of the discussion of single-morpheme utterances, however, a large question exists about the structure of these early sentences. Are they acquired as wholes with their underlying structure determined at some later stage of development, or has the child, at this stage, already acquired structures which allow him to generate utterances. The latter assumption seems to be more correct because of the patterns observed.

Some experimenters have termed these early two- or three-morpheme utterances as combinations of "pivot and open" classes." The very important observation that has been made is that the child seems to productively use rules for the combination of 'P's' and 'O's', and, thus, creates unique utterances. One of the primary postulations of the use of these rules is that one can derive sentences from O, P + O, O + P, and O + O but not P or P + P.[12] If we look at examples of these utterances we do not see a priori why these last two rules are not permissible (outside of the statement that they were not found in the language sample obtained). In addition, it has been stated that P may go to O and O to P in a child's system. If this is so, it is difficult to see how one can determine that the restriction rule is part of the child's grammar at this stage. More importantly, what is implicit in this description is that the child has classified the morphemes in his lexicon by placing them in either the category 'Open' or the category 'Closed.' Since, logically, classes are derived from functional relationships rather than relationships from classes it seems unlikely that the child has categorized the morphemes in his lexicon into classes (no matter how general) at this stage. The functional relationship expressed in these utterances seems to be that of subject or topic and predicate. The sentences produced at this stage of development invariably contain a morpheme which is the topic of the sentence and another morpheme which modifies the topic.

The utterances collected from a 20 months old boy during a half-hour of observation displayed these characteristics. There were many repetitions of the same utterance during this period which then led to overt testing of various combinations such as "mommy chair," "Ronnie chair," and Judy chair." This practice with language has been observed with other children[13] and seems to be the first indication of hypothesis testing in language acquisition. Thinking about language, at this stage of development, appears to be primarily overt. It should also be stated that some of the utterances directly followed mother's utterances. Sentences such as "Let's take your shoes off" were followed, somewhat later, by "shoe off" and "Oh! Your shoe fell" was followed by "shoe fall." However, they were not imitative. These utterances seem to be reformulations of the sentence in terms of the child's grammatical structures. Some of the lexical items in this child's utterances are like those collected by others,[14] in terms of traditional classifications, and some of them are not. Although there seems to be great similarity in the early utterances that have been collected thus far there is sufficient divergency to question the possibility of finding a hierarchy of acquisition in terms of traditional classifications of lexical items. In any case the Subject-Predicate relationship, the basic relationship in English, must be understood by the child before classes can be defined.

These first two morpheme utterances appear to be a topic plus a modifier.[15] Their underlying structure might be described in the following manner:

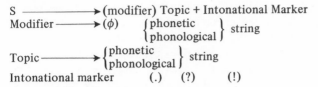

$$S \longrightarrow (\text{modifier}) \text{ Topic} + \text{Intonational Marker}$$
$$\text{Modifier} \longrightarrow (\phi) \quad \left\{ \begin{array}{l} \text{phonetic} \\ \text{phonological} \end{array} \right\} \text{ string}$$
$$\text{Topic} \longrightarrow \left\{ \begin{array}{l} \text{phonetic} \\ \text{phonological} \end{array} \right\} \text{ string}$$
$$\text{Intonational marker} \qquad (.) \quad (?) \qquad (!)$$

The order of modifier and topic is free in the utterances produced.

The utterances obtained during the above mentioned observation would then have the following derivations:

A.	*Modifier*	*Topic*	B.	*Topic*		*Modifier*
(I am)	big	boy		light	(is)	on
(I want)	more	milk		shoe	(is)	off
(I will)	go	car		Rick	(will)	go
(It did)	fall	down		shoe	(did)	fall
(You will)	pick	up				
(I will)	fix	shoe				
(This is)	mommy	chair				

In the description of the possible underlying structure of these utterances, modifiers have no further underlying structure but simply serve to express a relationship in these utterances. Modifiers, however, may be the Verb Phrase of the Predicate or the Noun Phrase of Predicates when the Copula is in the underlying structure. In addition to characterizing these utterances as Topic-Modifier constructions, the A group of sentences might be characterized as predicates and the B group of sentences (fewer in number) as Subject + Predicate if possible omissions, given the contextual information, are postulated as indicated in the parentheses above. We can do this, however, only if these omissions are assumed to be in the underlying structure of the sentences. The only category that seems to be missing is subjects alone. This is a reasonable omission if one assumes that during this period of development, language is not a referential system but an expression of overt acts. Subjects alone do not tell about overt acts. This kind of linguistic performance would fit Piaget's description of the thinking of the child during the sub period of preoperational thought. The child has been described during this period as an organism whose most intelligent functions are overt sensory-motor acts. At the end of this period the child's cognitions are inner symbolic manipulations of reality.[16]

When language is used to tell about observations, Subject + Predicate constructions would begin to appear.

The structural descriptions of possible base structure rules that have been presented in this discussion are obviously highly speculative. The problem is not that so few children have been observed during this period of development but that the descriptions have been limited to an observation of the patterns of combination of lexical items in these utterances. We can definitively state that the child does not simply repeat what he hears, although there are instances in which he will. At this age the child is using the items in his lexicon generatively to create new utterances. Outside of this very important observation, there is little known about this period. Two areas of research may add to our knowledge of what the child knows about language during this period. The first has already been mentioned in the discussion of single-morpheme utterances. The child's use of stress and intonational patterns may give us further knowledge of his linguistic competence. We do not know if all the morphemes in these two- or three-morpheme-length utterances are equally stressed or if they receive differential stress. It has been pointed out that application of stress is largely the result of the underlying structure of an utterance.[17] If this is the case the child's use of stress in these utterances may give us some evidence of the function of the different morphemes in these utterances. For example, we might find that the morphemes in utterances that have been postulated to be predicate structures would have unequal stress (mommy chair) whereas subject + predicate structures would have almost equal stress (shoe off). The second area of research is observation of the child's behavior when producing these utterances so that some evidence about the different functions of sentences when they are of a different shape can be obtained. Examination of the child's application of differing patterns of intonation and stress and observation of his behavior during the production of these utterances will give us evidence about the possible underlying structure of these utterances. We then may be able to describe the child's acquisition of the structure 'sentence,' his understanding and expression of functional relationships in sentences, and his definition of classes.

2.2 Development of Base Structure Rules

By age 3 all the children in this population used all the classes in base structure rules. At the same time sentences were produced which deviated from complete grammaticalness in the use of these base rules. The following is a sampling of the base structure rules which could be described from the sentences produced during the age range of 3 to 7:

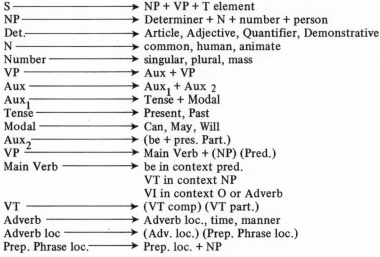

S ⟶ NP + VP + T element
NP ⟶ Determiner + N + number + person
Det. ⟶ Article, Adjective, Quantifier, Demonstrative
N ⟶ common, human, animate
Number ⟶ singular, plural, mass
VP ⟶ Aux + VP
Aux ⟶ Aux_1 + Aux_2
Aux_1 ⟶ Tense + Modal
Tense ⟶ Present, Past
Modal ⟶ Can, May, Will
Aux_2 ⟶ (be + pres. Part.)
VP ⟶ Main Verb + (NP) (Pred.)
Main Verb ⟶ be in context pred.
VT in context NP
VI in context O or Adverb
VT ⟶ (VT comp) (VT part.)
Adverb ⟶ Adverb loc., time, manner
Adverb loc ⟶ (Adv. loc.) (Prep. Phrase loc.)
Prep. Phrase loc. ⟶ Prep. loc. + NP

The underlying structure of the sentences produced by children can be described as expressing the following elements in the sample of rules given: grammatical relations (Subject-Object), syntactic order (Subject-Verb-Object), and syntactic classes (Noun, Verb, Determiner, etc.).

With these rules plus the use of the adjective transformation in sentences 2 through 5, sentences such as the following can be generated:

1. The boy saw the girl.
2. A boy saw the pretty girl.
3. The happy boy saw the pretty girl.
4. The happy boy saw the pretty girl yesterday.
5. The happy boy saw the pretty girl in the park yesterday.

Thus, we see that the nodes in the tree can be expanded in the derived structure of the sentence as, for example, Determiner going to Article + Adjective. However, the basic rules or structures of the sentence do not change. If NP only went to Noun there would be a basic difference in underlying structure because a class of the language would be eliminated. If VP only went to V there, again, would be a basic difference in underlying structure because the Subject-Object relationship could not be expressed.

We can see in the earlier sentences a gradual building up of base structure rules to define grammatical relations and grammatical classes. At the age we are observing now and with the children in this population the rules for a definition of these relations and classes have been acquired and, therefore, the term acquisition of basic syntactic structures in this component of the grammar is used. We shall now examine the sequence of acquisition of these structures.

The sentences that are produced during the first three quarters of the third year (2 years, 0 months to 2 years, 9 months) by two children, whose language was sampled once a month, indicate that the Subject-Predicate relationship is beginning to be more frequently expressed, rather than simply Predicate. However, Predicate constructions, with subjects not expressed but presumably in the underlying structure, still predominate during the early part of this period. Simultaneously, the classes of the language are beginning to be defined. If, for example, we examine this very sparse data for the development of the Noun Phrase into Determiner + Noun, Prepositional Phrase and Pronoun, certain gross developmental trends can be observed. The following are exemplars of structures at various age stages:

Determiner + Noun

2,1 to 3	Count a buttons.
	Wash a dishes.
2,4 to 7	Ere's a pencil.
	See dis name.
	No write this name.
	No hear a tapeacorder.
	This is sigareck, some candy sigareck.
2,8 to 9	How bout this part?
	Make anudder cake.
	I makin a cakes.
	I want the fire engines to talk.
	The monster's coming.

Two things can be observed in these utterances. First, the only determiner used in the earliest utterances is the indefinite Article 'a.' The demonstrative Determiner, 'this,' begins to appear shortly thereafter. Finally the definite Article, 'the,' appears. The quantifiers, 'some' and 'another' begin to appear at the end of the middle stage of this period. It should also be observed that the Determiner + Noun construction appears only in the predicate in the early months and not until the latter half of this period does it appear in the subject. Of course, Determiners are frequently not found at all in the sentences produced. The early use of the indefinite Article, 'a,' appears to be simply an inflection on the Noun. The very early use of the demonstrative Determiner, as compared to other possible Determiners, fits in very well with the hypothesis that language at this stage of development is being used as an expression of overt acts, rather than as a referential system. The parceling out of the distinct properties of Determiners and constraints on their use with Nouns continues for some time as can be seen in the utterances produced by older children. However, this latter task is very different from that which is accomplished at this stage. Now, the child is in the process of acquiring a class in the language, whereas at later stages, he is analyzing how the class is used in specific contexts in his language. The development of this class in the language seems to be first a general observation, perhaps simply phonological (something appears before topics), which is applied generatively and sometimes inappropriately. Then the child expresses a particular instance of a topic that he is dealing with at the moment. This also seems to be the case in the development of Prepositional Phrases.

Prepositional Phrases

2,0 to 3	Daddy uh New York.
	Mommy sit uh table.
	Bottle/bottle uh bed.
2,4 to 7	Put a pencil in dair.
	Put in head.
	Going on floor.
	It fell in sand box.
	I just take the sand off my shoe.
2,8 to 9	He's going up in the ladder.
	Talk to mommy on the tape recorder.
	I can get out of there.
	The guy's gonna knock it down all to the house.

We observe in the very early utterances that a neutral vowel sound, 'uh,' is being used. Again, this appears to be a phonological observation that is used generatively but in a very different manner than the indefinite article. The indefinite Article is most frequently found in the context Verb____ Noun, whereas the Preposition is most frequently found in the context N(Verb)____N. This indicates that although the actual utterances may sound alike ('uh'), their underlying structure is quite different. We see developing simultaneously Verb + Particle ('put in' and 'take off') and the Prepositional Phrase ("Daddy uh New York," "It fell in sandbox," and "I can get out of here"). All of these constructions indicate place, which is the most overt use of Prepositions and Particles. Prepositional Phrases of manner and time do not begin to appear until some time later. Within each category (place, time, and manner) the exact prepositional morpheme to be used in the Noun Phrase context must be determined. Therefore, we see at this stage of development and at a later stage inappropriate use of the Preposition and Particle ("Put in head" and "He's going up in the ladder"). The more frequent use by these two children of the Preposition and Particle 'in' as compared to others is intriguing. However, until many more children than two are observed, and in experimental situations, our speculations about the development of the classes already discussed and of the Pronoun to be discussed must be very general. One can only observe that the use of Prepositions and Particles at this stage of development is, again, limited to verbalizing about overt acts.

Pronouns

2,0 to 3   Mommy try it.
            Cut it.
            Nose hurt you.

2,4 to 7   No—show you mommy.
            Turn it off the light.
            Eric close it mommy's lap.
            I making cake too.

2,8 to 9   You knock down the snow.
            I show you again.
            Here she is.
            He's gonna talk.

In the earlier utterances Pronoun usage is limited to 'it' and always in the Predicate. For some time this is the only Pronoun used. The utterance "Nose hurt you" is an exceptional use of 'you' during the early part of this period, and is in response to "Does your nose hurt you?" It is included to indicate that occurrence of Pronouns other than 'it' at this time appear to be simply repetitions rather than generated uses. This, of course, occurs with members of the other classes that have been discussed.

When speaking of themselves these children use their proper names instead of 'I.' When speaking to another person in the situation their proper name or title ('mommy') is used rather than 'you.' It is only in the latter part of this period that Pronoun Subjects are found. The early use of 'it' may simply be an inflection on the Verb, or it may be the root for the Noun Phrase 'something.' At the middle stage of development the 'it' is being used to refer to something as is indicated by the fact that its reference is often conjoined to the sentence ("Turn it off the light"). The use of Pronouns to refer to persons, however, does not appear until the last stage of this period. Again, this seems to be evidence that language during the early part of this period is used to express overt acts rather than as a referential system.

The development of the Verb Phrase during this period takes two directions. One is the development of morphological markers for tense and number and the other is the acquisition of the auxiliary and modal Verbs. These two aspects of Verb Phrase development in older children will be discussed in the sections on morphology and transformations, respectively.

However, it should be stated now that the progression in this limited data seems to be from Verb to Verb + present progressive to Verb + past to Aux be/Modal + Verb. Although there are utterances at the early period of development which indicate the presence of an auxiliary ("Mommy's shaking pencil"), the more frequent occurrence during the early months of this period and somewhat later are utterances such as "Marie writing name" and "I making cake too." If we hypothesize that, at the beginning of this stage of development, language is being used primarily as an expression of overt acts there should be no tense distinction since the only time is now. It should be kept in mind that these are speculations about the sentences produced and the underlying structure that one may describe for these utterances, based on production alone. We do not know, for example, whether or not the child comprehends differences in times of occurrence either before or after he has acquired the appropriate verbal productions.

It has often been stated, in general terms, that young children's language is "concrete" rather than "abstract." The use of the term "concrete" seems misleading. The statement has been based, in large part, on the properties of the Nouns in children's lexicons. In some sense children's sentences are more "abstract" than those of adults since more aspects in children's sentences are unspecified. One can, somewhat more definitively, state that the young child's total grammar, the functional relationships expressed in his utterances and his definition of classes, seems to be used to generate expressions of overt acts. He must 'select' this grammar since the language that he hears does not isolate or present it to him. There seems to be a striking similarity between this description of his linguistic performance and descriptions of his cognitive performance at this stage.

In the age range of 3 to 4 years, where numbers of children have been observed, the syntactic classes have been acquired, and the various members of a class are, to a large extent, all being used, although, in some instances inappropriately. The developmental trend that is notable in the sentences that are produced during this period and later is an increasing competence in observation of selectional constraints on the cooccurrence of members of these classes.

We indicated earlier that with these rules and continuous branching of the underlying structure very elaborate sentences can be generated. For example, 'the happy boy' could be expanded into 'the happy, clever, handsome (etc.) boy.' In this manner an indefinitely long string can be generated. No actually produced sentence is indefinitely long since we are limited by the restrictions of our memory capacity and the decreasing utility of such a procedure in communication. However, the use of this aspect of the grammar is a savings. Instead of saying 'The boy is happy' then

'The boy is clever' then 'The boy is handsome' and then 'The boy was a success,' we can say 'The happy, clever, handsome boy was a success.' We can use this savings device of multiple branching up to the limit of our memory capacity. A primary motivation for the acquisition of multiple branching rules would be, then, the savings gained by the use of these types of rules. The acquisition of transformational rules might be partially motivated by the economy they introduce. For example, in the use of conjunction rules we can also generate indefinitely long sentences. 'I see a comb,' 'I see a brush,' 'I see nail polish,' etc., becomes "I see a comb, (a) brush, nail polish, (etc.)"

What has frequently been noted about the child's language development is that his mean sentence length increases as he matures. We can see in the examples given above that by continuous expansion of base structure rules, and the use of conjunction, sentence length is increased. However, mean sentence length per se does not measure increasing grammatical sophistication or, rather, only the surface aspects of it in some instances. In other instances, as has been noted before, mean sentence length may be measuring personality and situational differences rather than grammatical competence. Once having acquired the basic rules that NP can be expanded into Determiner + Noun, and VP can be expanded into V + NP, and that S can be expanded into $S_1 + S_2$ with possible deletions, the child has acquired the rules for generating indefinitely long sentences. Mean sentence length can be deceiving as a measure of grammatical competence. Using the rules of conjunction a child can generate a longer sentence by producing, for example, (1) 'I see a brush and I see a comb' than he does by applying deletion rules to generate (2) 'I see a brush, comb and nail polish' with Subject and Verb understood to apply to 'comb' and 'nail polish.' Yet sentence 2, although shorter in length, indicates that the child has acquired an additional rule and indicates that he has deepened his analysis of the grammar further than does the production of sentence 1. In terms of this discussion, production of the shorter sentence indicates greater grammatical competence than does production of the longer sentence. The effect of personality and situational differences on mean sentence length will not be discussed here since it is the generalizations that one can make about developing grammatical competence that is the topic of this discussion, rather than individual differences. One could note, however, that children differ in their linguistic style as do adults and that, further, style is affected by situation. For this reason, within a given time sampling of language, one may find some children who generate lengthier sentences than do other children, but, as the examples given show, the lengthier sentences need not necessarily involve more complex or even different underlying structures than shorter sentences.

An aspect of the continuing grammatical development that takes place during the age range of this population is use of elaborated forms of basic rules. One notes, over the age range observed, an expansion of the nodes in the base structure string. One also observes a collapsing of several sentences into one. Both these factors are related. Looking at a picture in the set of Blacky Pictures the following types of comments are made by children at younger and older ages:

Younger   Age 3,11 "I see a house. It's made of wood."
Older   Age 5,11 "I see a wooden house."
Younger   Age 4,11 "I see a house and another and another."
Older   Age 6,0   "I see three houses."

The principle involved is one of remembering rules and properties in the base structure string. In the expanded structure of, for example, (Article, Adjective, Adjective, Adjective) + Noun, it must be remembered that each item in the parenthesized set refers to the Noun and is restricted by the Noun. In the operations of conjunction and deletion it must be remembered that the same NP + V of S_1 applies to S_2, S_3, etc.[18] One must remember, in fact, the underlying structure or derivation of the expanding and collapsing procedure.

If the child has acquired a set of rules for the generation of a structure he may continuously apply this same set of rules in the manner cited. In the continuous application of the same set of rules he must remember that each addition requires restrictions. In acquiring a basic syntactic structure the child must remember the complete set of rules needed to derive this structure. In generating an elaboration of a basic syntactic structure the child must remember to apply his complete set of rules to each elaboration. It is probably for these reasons that younger children use simpler basic syntactic structures than do older children, and younger children use elaborations of basic syntactic structures less frequently than do older children. One aspect, then, of maturation in grammatical competence might be described as 'increasing memory capacity.' This is not increasing memory capacity in terms of sentence length or number of morphemes in a sentence but, rather, increasing memory capacity for basic structures and elaborated structures which require an increasingly differentiated and larger number of rules for their generation. It must be remembered that all these comments about competence have thus far been based on a description of performance. This subject will be discussed further in the chapter on grammatical competence.

While all the children in this sample were using all the syntactic classes which can be described in base structure rules, they were, simultaneously, using these rules in ways which in some instances deviated from complete grammaticalness.

This observation is quite different from stating that the child has not, as yet, acquired a syntactic class. If there is no instance or very few instances (that is, randomly) in which the child produces Determiner + Noun with a Determiner of any kind (Article, Adjective, or Quantifier, etc.) then one can state the child has not acquired the rule NP —➤Determiner + Noun, on the productive level in any case. However, in observing the children of this age range it was found, for example, that they were producing many instances of the above rule. It is only sometimes that deviations from the completely grammatical form of this rule were produced. Therefore, one can state that they have acquired the rule but do not use the complete rule in all instances.

Some deviations seem to be exemplars of the creativity of children in using the language and their observation that the same word can be lexically categorized in several ways. Although the stems of these words are usually in a different lexical class than the one in which they are being used by the children, there is, nevertheless, application of correct syntactic rules for their use in particular sentences. An example is, "I see the hungries," where Adjective becomes Noun but with the correct application of the morphological rules for Noun, plural. Another example is, "His tail is flagging," where Noun becomes Verb but with the correct present participle ending for the verb. We do not find, at this age, violations of lexical class in which there is substitution without modification. Even this modified form of deviation appears with much less frequency after the nursery school period.

There are also certain violations of subcategorization rules which seem different in nature to the ones we will be discussing. Most of these violations are concerned with Adjective + Noun constructions: "He's a bigger," "I want the blue," "Give me the last." Others are the possessive form of Adjective + Noun: "I took them to the doctor's," "I'm playing Billie's." However, most of these forms do not seem particularly deviant, (with the possible exception of utterances such as "He's a bigger"), especially not in conversation where the Noun of the Adjective + Noun construction may have been referred to previously or the noun is predictable as in 'doctor's (office),' or 'Joanie's (house).' Some of these ellipses seem permissible and do not appear to be deviant in the same way as an utterance such as "This candy tastes" seems to be. It would be interesting to explore experimentally those ellipses which seem permissible to children and those which do not. A possible reason for the frequency of usage of seemingly permissible ellipses in the productions of children is presented in the discussion on transformations.

There are also violations of ordering in strings. They are primarily inversions of object to the subject position and they occur throughout the age range. Some examples are the following:

1. Brothers and sisters I have.
2. All the letters of A.B.C. I don't know.
3. Some more cat I make.
4. Hisself Blacky talks to.
5. This one you have to paste.
6. His paw he has to put up.

These inversions occur despite the fact that, according to Greenberg,[19] Subject always precedes Object in a number of languages. One finds sequences such VSO, SVO and SOV but not, as in the above instances, OSV. The rule in operation in these sentences seems to be always S + V with O position optional. These sentences are easily understood and do not seem very nongrammatical. If the Verb as well as the Object were inverted, sentences 1-4 would seem somewhat more deviant but not very much so. Sentences 5 and 6 on the other hand would seem quite deviant if the Verb inversion took place: 'This one have to paste you' and "His paw has to put up he.' Two factors seem to be in operation. In sentences 1-4 the Subject-Object relationship is clearly marked either by the Pronoun 'I' or by the reflexive. This is also true of sentences 5 and 6 but in these sentences the subject is more distant from the main Verb by the interpolation of the Infinitival Complement. Of primary importance for clarity of interpretation is the closeness of Subject + main Verb, and this is reflected in the inversions that are found in children's language samples and those which are not. The Verb as well as Object inversions are not found in the language sample. The ordering SOV which would separate the Subject and main Verb is also not found in the language sample ('I brothers and sisters have.').

The study of children's rules of ordering should be further explored. Asking them to repeat sentences with SVO, SOV, OSV, and OVS orders and recording their responses and asking them to identify the Subject and Object in sentences of varying order ('Blacky talks to himself,' 'Blacky himself talks to,' 'Himself Blacky talks to,' and 'Himself talks to Blacky') are possible approaches to this exploration.

Outside of the above mentioned deviations most of the deviations observed could be classified into three categories. The first category is nonexpansion of a symbol in the string, or omission. The second category is conflict with selectional restrictions, a violation of a strict subcategorization rule, or substitution. The third category is further expansion of a terminal symbol in the string, or redundancy.

Nonexpansion of a symbol in the base structure string occurs with any syntactic class. It occurs more frequently with some classes than with others and sometimes only in specific contexts. The following are descriptions of the nonexpansions observed:

Noun Phrase[20]

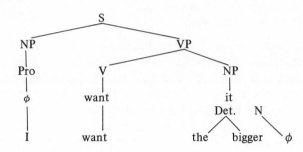

Verb Phrase[21]

Preposition

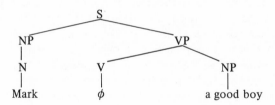

Determiner

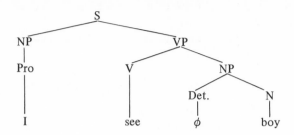

Particle

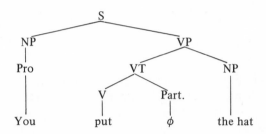

The second category of deviation is conflict with selectional features or with restrictions placed on cooccurrence of lexical items in a string. Selectional restrictions are not always observed in choice of Determiner + Noun, Noun + Verb, Preposition + NP, and Pronoun + NP in a string. It has been stated that the Nouns dominate the Verb, its Determiner, the Preposition in a Prepositional Phrase, and the Pronoun in Copula + Predicate Nominal sentences. However, in some instances it is not clear that it is the Noun which imposes restrictions on all other parts of the string. The following are examples of structures found in the language sample of the population which could be described as nonobservation of selectional restrictions.

Pronoun— In the use of the Pronoun the properties of the Noun Phrase of the Verb Phrase are not always observed.[22]
He's a big train— Train is inanimate
She's a nice daddy— 'Daddy' is male
It's a good boy— 'Boy' is human

Verb– In the use of Verbs the properties of the Noun Phrase of the sentence or the Noun Phrase of the Verb Phrase or the Verb of the Verb Phrase are not always observed.

The water is hanging down– Properties of water not observed.

My daddy takes a shave every day– Properties of 'shave' or of 'take' not observed.[23]

She does the flowers– properties of 'does' not observed[24]

Determiner– In the use of determiners the properties of the Noun in any Noun Phrase are sometimes not observed.

A blue leaves–The nouns are plural.

This things

So much pictures

A Billy– The noun is proper.

These grass– The noun is mass.

A milk

Some piece _ The noun is singular.
All the car

Preposition– In the use of Prepositions the properties of the Noun Phrase of the Prepositional Phrase or the Noun Phrase of the Verb Phrase are not observed. In other instances the properties of the main Verb + Object are not observed.[25]

She's a nurse at the daytime.

He'll be 3 in June 10th.

They went to stay at the puppy.

He's pointing his finger to it.

He took me at the circus.

There were no instances in which selection restrictions were not observed in the use of Particles although they were observed at an earlier stage of development (as in "Put in head"). One did not find in this population, for example, such constructions as 'look on this.' A frequent production, however, was "look it" in the Imperative construction. In most Particle constructions one has the option of applying the separation transformation as in 'Put on the hat,' or 'Put the hat on.' The only instance in which the transformation is obligatory is with Pronoun Objects: 'Put it on' and 'Take her away' but not 'Put on it' and 'Take away her.' With this set of Verbs many varying types of constructions are possible: 'put off,' 'put over,' 'take on,' 'take over,' 'take off.' Therefore, this set may be acquired as Verb + Particle, and, as we have noted, omissions of the Particle occur ('Put the hat'). On the other hand there is a set of Verbs, such as 'look,' with which the separation transformation never occurs. We say 'Look at the book' but not 'Look the book at.' What may occur with this set is that its members are learned as whole Verbs rather than Verb + Particle and therefore are used as any other Verb. 'Look it,' with 'it' in place of 'at' seems to be merely a phonological rule application of vowel reduction. 'Look it' then may be simply an alternate form of the Verb 'look.' Despite the fact that the data on this aspect of grammar acquisition are presently quite limited, the point is worthy of discussion and should be examined much more carefully, since it appears to be a good example of the kinds of generalizations children seem capable of making from quite complicated linguistic data.

As the child more consistently expands his Noun Phrases and Verb Phrases and increases the variety of Nouns and Verbs that he uses, the number of selectional restrictions involved in the generation of a sentence, of course, also increases. When he is consistently expanding Noun Phrase into Determiner + Noun and Verb Phrase into Verb + Prepositional Phrase we first begin to note that certain selectional restrictions are not always observed. If, for example, the child is using only concrete Nouns at a certain stage of development, the selectional restrictions involved in the use of Determiners and Verbs with abstract Nouns need not be applied. It is only when he begins to use the class Noun, abstract, that we begin to note that certain selectional restrictions are not always observed. As a gain is made in expansion and diversification of structures there seems to be always a period in which one can observe deviations from the completely grammatical form of this expansion or diversification. It is as if the child has a testing period for a particular acquisition to see how well his hypotheses fit the linguistic data.

The interesting questions about this period of acquisition and development in base structure rules are not concerned with size of vocabulary. This, like mean sentence length, is a surface aspect of the underlying structure of the child's grammar. We would like to describe this underlying structure to gain some insight into the linguistic processes by which the child organizes his experience. We are interested in (1) the properties of the morphemes in his lexicon at certain stages of development, and (2) the acquisition, in time, of selectional restriction rules concerning the use of morphemes with particular properties. We observe, at the earliest stages, that the child uses animate and inanimate Nouns (bed, doggie), and animate animal and human Nouns (kittie, Billy) but we have not, through the procedure of observation of the production of these morphemes, determined that these properties have indeed been isolated and marked by the child for use in sentences. Use of the generic term (animal, man, furniture, food) also does not guarantee that the properties of these classes have been marked for syntactic use. We notice in fact that generic terms are sometimes used inappropriately ("I got new furnitures"). However, when selectional restrictions, which must be applied across morpheme boundaries, are applied, perhaps we can begin to assume that certain properties are on their way to being isolated. (For example, when one notes that the child produces 'milk is,' not 'are'; 'people take,' not 'desks'; 'animals eat,' not 'chairs,' we may assume that the properties of number and animacy are beginning to be understood and applied in sentences.) One must also be careful to isolate difficulty with a particular labeling system from a nonunderstanding of properties. For example, number is marked in several ways. We mark the Noun as singular and plural, we mark the Verb in present tense third person as singular and plural, and we make a distinction in the Article. We cannot state that because a child produces "A leaves fall from the tree" that he doesn't understand the properties of singular and plural but only, as in the above examples, that he doesn't *always* observe the selectional restrictions in the use of Articles with plural Nouns.

In summary, simple classification into generic categories as exhibited in the production of certain morphemes will not suffice to satisfy us about the child's understanding of the properties of the morphemes he uses. Examination of the selectional restrictions that the child observes in his use of these morphemes in sentences gives us additional and more valid information about the child's understanding of properties. However, we have as yet very little data on this most important aspect of linguistic development. As was stated, in the population of this study, on occasion, selectional restrictions were not observed, but for the most part they were. In addition, the examples given above lump together understanding of properties and observation of properties in the generation of strings. Experiments to determine which violations of selectional restrictions are acceptable and which are not at various stages of development is one possible approach to a formal description of this aspect of grammar.

The third category of deviation is further expansion of a terminal symbol in the string. One can observe these deviations with Noun Phrases, Verb Phrases, Determiners, Prepositions, and Particles. The following are some examples:

Noun Phrase

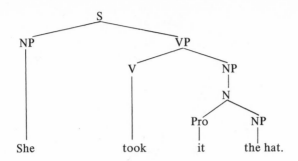

Verb Phrase

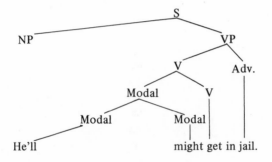

Determiner

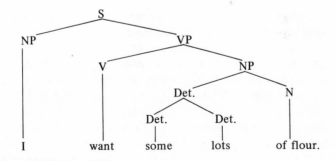

Particle

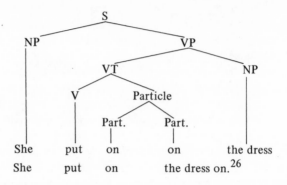

Preposition

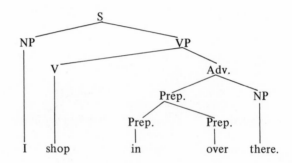

We have again grossly categorized probably several phenomena. In some sense one can state that these deviations are violations of selectional restrictions, that is, of what can appear in what context. However, they are qualitatively different from the deviations noted earlier, in the second category, since each Noun of the redundant Noun Phrase, each modal of the redundant Verb Phrase, etc., is used appropriately. What seems to be occurring is further expansion of a symbol to insure understanding of the listener or greater definition. At first glance these sentences might also appear to be conjunction of sentences with radical ellipses or another form of the conjunction of Noun Phrase and sentence noted in earlier sentences in the following manner: She took it away + She took away the hat ⟶ She took it away the hat. He'll get in jail + He might get in jail ⟶ He'll might get in jail. I want some flour + I want lots of flour ⟶ I want some lots of flour. She put on the dress + She put the dress on ⟶ She put on the dress on. I shop in there + I shop over there ⟶ I shop in over there.

Although we might formally describe these productions in this way, several interrelated factors would lead us to believe that they are operationally different and structurally better described as further expansions of terminal symbols. The first factor is that this third category of deviation occurs most frequently in the latter part of the age range (first grade) when a great leap in expansion of basic structures and the addition of new structures by greater numbers of children is occurring. The trend is toward greater definition by expansion of structures. Second, the technique of conjunction and permissible deletions has been well accomplished by this time. Third, the redundancies occur in completely well-formed sentences with the reiteration of a particular class. Fourth, the previously observed pause between sentence and addition is not observed in these sentences. For example, one does not hear 'I want some, lots of flour.'

The statement has been made that the grammars of languages are inefficient because of their unnecessary complexity and high degree of redundancy. The idea that the grammars of languages are arbitrary in structure, that is, subject to random change and with more exceptions than rules, has been, to a great extent, disproven by descriptions of the underlying orderliness of grammars which generate seemingly arbitrary outputs if one looks only at surface structure. It is the conception of the unnecessary complexities and the redundancies in language which has led theorists to postulate that a need-oriented hypothesis of language acquisition is not borne out by the facts observed. There is no necessity to contend with the intricacies of a fully developed grammar when one can reduce hunger, thirst, etc., with a minimal grammar, which may, in fact, consist of cries, gestures, or single-morpheme sentences. Setting aside a need hypothesis based on a primary drive reduction, it has been hypothesized that the child has a need to understand and convey more specific meaning in an expanding environment. This may be, in part, correct. However, it still does not account for the fact that a grammar that is both complex and highly redundant is acquired. It has been observed that, over time, changes may be introduced into a language to decrease its complexity and redundancy. These changes may possibly be introduced by new generations of children. In other instances changes in the language may increase its redundancy and complexity. There seems to be no language which can substantially be described as being simpler than another. It is possible, therefore, that the redundancies in a language are necessary to the human organism in dealing with a verbal symbol system. The simplest hypothetical grammar, that is, one which conveys all possible meanings with the fewest number of rules, none of which creates redundancies, may not be the most efficient for the human organism. For example, to mark number (singular or plural) once in a string may not be sufficient for the continuous and rapid decoding of a string. In the real grammar of English, number is always marked more than once: 'He (sing.) plays (sing.)' or 'They (plural) play (plural)' or 'a (sing.) boy (sing.) plays (sing.).'

The further expansions of terminal symbols may be introduced by the child to create redundancies in the string, and, thus, ensure that the structures he wishes to generate are fully understood.

It should be stated again that the deviations that have been discussed occur infrequently in the language sample collected. Further, no child consistently produced an incomplete form in base structure rules, thereby indicating that certain classes that have been described had not as yet been acquired. Certain rules of cooccurrence were sometimes not observed, but in other instances they were. These incomplete forms were only produced in alternation with the completely grammatical form. These deviations are indications of processes which occur in grammatical development after basic rules have been acquired. In Figure 2.1 the mean percentage of the children in the three groups who are using the three categories of incomplete rules with all syntactic classes is plotted to indicate developmental trends.

Overall the numbers of children producing these forms is reduced over the age range. Nonexpansion of a terminal symbol in the string occurs most frequently in the nursery school group. Nonobservation of selectional restrictions occurs most frequently in the nursery school and kinder-

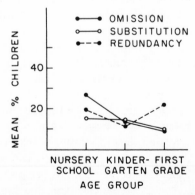

Figure 2.1 Mean percentage of children using rules with omissions, substitutions, and redundancies in base structures in nursery school, kindergarten, and first grade.

garten groups and is the category of deviation that occurs most frequently in the kindergarten group. Further expansion of a terminal symbol occurs most frequently in the first grade group.

We were interested in seeing what types of deviant rules individual children were using within the groups as well as the types of deviant rules the groups as a whole used. Many more of the children in all groups used a *single type* of deviant rule with a syntactic class than a combination of deviant rules. That is, significantly more of the children were either at the stage of omitting or substituting or using a syntactic class redundantly rather than omitting and substituting the same class or substituting and using the same class redundantly, etc. The percentages of children using a single or multiple type of deviant rule within the three groups are given in Table 2.1. P values were obtained by χ^2 evaluation.

We were also interested in noting the rank order of the syntactic classes in terms of the percentages of children who were producing these classes with deviant rules, and, also, which type of deviant rule was used by the greatest number of children with each class in each group. Table 2.2 lists the syntactic classes in order of percentages of children in the total population and in each group who generate these classes with deviant rules from

Table 2.1

Percentage of Children Using Single or Multiple Types of Deviant Rule within the Groups with Base Structure Rules

Group	Single %	P Value	Multiple %
N.S.	70	.01	13
Kinder	46	.01	10
First Grade	50	.01	9

Table 2.2

Rank Order of Syntactic Classes Used with Deviant Rules by Total Population and Each Group

R.O.	Total	% Type	N.S.	% Type	Kinder	% Type	First G.	% Type
1	N P	70 R	NP	76 O	NP	63 S	NP	70 R
2	Prep	45 R	Prep	55 R	VP	48 S	Prep	45 R
3	VP	43 S	VP	50 S	Prep	35 S	VP	30 S
4	Det	31 O	Det	46 O	Det	23 O	Det	23 R
5	Part	12 O	Part	27 O	Part	6 O	Part	4 R

greatest to least. The symbol under the heading 'type' denotes the type of deviant rule most frequently used by the group for each class; O = omission, S = substitution, and R = redundancy.

As can be seen in Table 2.2, Nouns or Pronouns are the syntactic class most frequently produced with deviant rules. However, the type of deviant rule used varies within the groups. In the nursery school group more children do not expand the Noun symbol in the string. In the kindergarten group more children do not observe the selectional restrictions in expanding the symbol. In the first grade group more children further expand the terminal symbol in the string. The next two classes most frequently produced with deviant rules are Prepositions and Verbs. Verbs are most frequently produced without observing the selectional restrictions on their use in a string by all three groups, and the Preposition symbol is further expanded most frequently by all three groups. Determiners and Particles are most frequently omitted by the nursery school and kindergarten group and are most frequently used redundantly by the first grade group. These are the observable facts.

2.3 Semantics

We would like to discuss these observations in terms of the context in which they occur and another aspect of grammar—semantic properties of symbols in kernel strings and semantic rules. The fact that the connection between the form and the meaning of a word is arbitrary might again raise the question that was posed earlier. Is the fact that the child does not make certain differentiations and observe certain selectional restrictions, dependent on properties of symbols, in his production of language, an indication that he has perceptually and cognitively not as yet made these differentiations? It may also be that in some instances he is using the proper terms but has not as yet made the necessary perceptual and cognitive differentiations. This is a trying question—one which has occupied a great many psychologists and linguists. We shall not attempt to parcel it out because, as was indicated, mere observation of what is produced cannot give us conclusive answers. However, some speculation based on an analysis of available data, may give us some insight into the processes involved in the acquisition of meaning of words and the use of words in strings, and perhaps indicate areas for further research.

Looking at the sentences produced, the most frequent occurrence of nonexpansion of the Noun symbol in the nursery school group seems to be in the context Pronoun where Pronoun goes to zero: "Give O the clay," "Don't throw O on my shoes," "We know how to fix O," etc. The most frequent occurrence of nonobservation of selectional restrictions in the kindergarten group is in the context Pronoun: 'it for 'she,' 'it' for 'father,' 'it' for 'he,' it' for 'shoes,' etc. On occasion one finds Noun substitution of derived Nominalizations such as, "I didn't see any reading on that," and confusions in form such as "He cooks chemists." The most frequent occurrence of further expansion of the terminal symbol in the first grade group is in the same context, Pronoun: "I want it the brush," "He Blacky washed hisself," etc.

The gender, number, and case aspects of Pronouns are arbitrarily applied by specific morpheme labels rather than rule and, therefore, it might be stated that this discussion belongs in the section on morphological rules. However, since the Pronoun, when employed, is either the Noun Phrase of the sentence or the Noun Phrase of the Verb Phrase (Subject or Object), this aspect of grammatical development seems to belong properly in the discussion of base structure rules. The following observations can be made about the development of this subclass in addition to the comments that were made about the beginning stages of the acquisition of this subclass. The Pronoun is most frequently used in contexts in which the reference is completely understood: "(I) want it," "(You) take it," "Give (me) the kittie." In some sense the Pronoun is redundant since its reference is clear. At these beginning stages one finds, therefore, that the Pronoun is frequently omitted. At a later stage when this subclass is more frequently used in contexts in which the reference is not always clear (the reference may have been mentioned several sentences back, or it may be the Object of the sentence or the Subject of sentence 1 of a conjunction of two sentences, etc.), the properties of number and gender are not always observed. As was noted the most frequent substitution is the neuter Pronoun 'it,' although 'she' for 'he' and vice versa are also found. At a still later stage, and, because of the previous types of occurrences, Pronouns may be a tenuous class in a sentence. Therefore, at this stage, Pronouns are redefined or more clearly distinguished by adding the Noun referent. The context in which this most frequently occurs is with 'it' as Object. The process seems to be increasing definition and differentiation of a tenuous subclass. It is little wonder that observers have found that children frequently have difficulty in using this subclass in a completely grammatical form in sentences. We do not think that the usual difficulty lies in differentiating oneself from the rest of the world or conceptually differentiating gender and number as has often been postulated, but, rather, primarily in the obscure syntactic role this subclass plays in sentence.

Verb Phrase substitution is the next deviant rule in the rank order of usage of deviant rules. This deviancy was discussed briefly in the general discussion of base structure rules, but we would now like to speculate about why this deviant rule occurs with such frequency. If we look at some of the most frequent kinds of Verb Phrase substitution we see certain clusters of the kind indicated below. The arrows indicate the direction of substitutions and we have tried to find a possible title for a clustering.

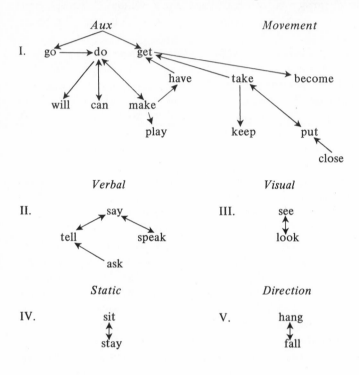

To use De Saussure's terminology[27] "semantic fields" seem to be described by these clusterings. What might possibly be occurring is that members of each cluster have at some level of development equal properties and are nondifferentiated. At the age range we are observing we cannot state that this is the case since these substitutions occur infrequently in the total population and by an individual child. However, it may be that objects, space, and time are a point at one stage of development which expands to include many different terms which are considered to be alike and then are specifically differentiated. That is, several types of operations are occurring in terms of the acquisition of properties of symbols. Symbols at one stage may imply a single instance: 'chair' may be a single chair and no others. Symbols at another stage may imply a nondifferentiated group: 'chair' may include a table and chair, etc. A group of symbols may be used but they imply only one generalization: 'chair' and 'table' may mean 'chair.' For example, some Russian researchers have found in their analysis of the child's acquisition of space terminology that although both the terms of 'right' and 'left' are used at a certain stage, both imply only right.[28] Finally, symbols are used appropriately: 'chair' implies those objects which have the attributes of chair only. At some point in development the child has the capacity to acquire new lexical items without following the sequence of stages or any part of it by simply observing the meaning of a new morpheme through environmental and syntactic context and a knowledge of the semantic rules incorporated in his grammar.

This brings us to the question of how meaning is learned. The meaning of words might be learned as a referential system by observing that certain words are used to refer to certain objects. However, in the following example and in many other examples, single word reference does not suffice to acquire meaning. The word 'walk' could, in general terms, mean either (1) a cleared space leading to the front door of a house, (2) an action involved in moving one's feet, or (3) to move one's feet one after the other. In instances 1 and 2 the word is a Noun and in instance 3, a Verb. The various meanings of a single word have to be learned from *syntactic context.:* "The walk is red brick" (N1), "Take a walk" (N2), and "I walk very fast" (V1). Even in terms of easily seen single objects, reference has to be parceled out when the phonetic sequences representing these objects are in connected speech (a cat, a caterpillar, a cat, or pillow are soft). This can be done only by understanding the underlying syntactic structure. There are sentences which are ambiguous such as, "The walk was long." (Is it N1 or N2?) In this case the sentence may be disambiguated by situational context. The hearer refers to learned syntactic context and properties to disambiguate the sentence and decide on whether it is N1 or N2. The child, therefore, must learn both the properties of words and, in addition to this, he must observe the restrictions attendant on the relationships of words in sentences in order to derive meanings. The following examples indicate that children in this age range are not observing all the properties of morphemes and the restrictions attendant on cooccurrence of morphemes having these properties in sentences.

They'll close him in jail.
I want to say in the microphone.
He does instruments.
She has to make a lot of work.
I didn't see at the other pictures.

The percentage of children using Preposition redundancy ranks high among the percentages of children using all types of deviant rules in all three groups. The reason for this may be a general ambivalency about appropriate selection of Prepositions. There is difficulty in determining the correct Preposition to denote place, manner, and time in specific contexts as well. Although further expansion of a terminal symbol ranks highest, nonobservation of selectional restrictions ranks a close second in all three groups (17 percent versus 11 percent). Nonexpansion of the Preposition symbol occurs much less frequently than the other two types of deviant rules even at the nursery school level.

Another explanation is that various terms for place, manner, and time have not as yet been either acquired in some instances or, in other instances, are not clearly defined. Therefore, one finds an elaboration of terms to give finer definition to the available Prepositions ("He gets all the way close" for, possibly, 'almost near') and an elaboration of terms because a member of the term is not clearly understood ("He went beside from the house" for simply 'beside'). Frequent use in completely grammatical form of 'during,' 'near,' 'beside,' 'between,' etc., is not found. An earlier stage of development might be more frequent use of substitute Prepositions ("She wants to stay at the puppy," "She goes to it on the night time," "He's going on a rush.") After certain members of this class are a part of the child's dictionary he may use them conjointly to attempt to express meanings for which he has not yet acquired the appropriate lexical items.

In the use of Determiner and Particles, nonexpansion of the terminal symbol is the most frequent type of deviant rule found with nursery school and kindergarten children. On the other hand, further expansion of the terminal symbol is the most frequent type of deviant rule used with these classes by the oldest group of children: the first grade group. We see here a very good example of the developmental trend in the continuing process of attempting to achieve greater and greater definition with language. The nonexpansion of the terminal symbol creates ambiguities as in the following sentences:

It blowed the window. (in?, out?, down?, etc.)
Do we put this? (here?, there?, down?, etc.)

The further expansion of the terminal symbol assures nonambiguity as in the following sentences:

The barber cut off his hair off.
Put on some rouge on.

In addition to the above instances there are relatively frequent occurrences in the first grade group where Particle is added unnecessarily to the Verb as in the following utterances:

He's biting it up.
He shaved up again.
Those trains bumped in.
The cars crashed in.
They didn't look out where they were going.

These do not seem to be ellipses of possibly longer sentences. One might say "The cars crashed in to each other," but we do not know what the continuation of "He's biting it up" could possibly be. These utterances seem just one more instance of additions to achieve greater definition.

Once a rule for the expansion of a base structure symbol has been acquired (the acquisition of a class), the next step seems to be expansion of the set of members of this class. Acquisition of a class is a syntactic development whereas expansion of the set in a class is both a semantic and a syntactic development. Lexical items with appropriate semantic as well as syntactic properties are added to the dictionary. At the earliest stages of development in this period, sentences are sometimes produced without any member of a class although the structure of the sentence makes the production of the class obligatory. This appears to be nonobservation of a syntactic rule rather than nonobservation of a semantic rule. There are some members of a class which are acquired before others. The semantic properties of those members which are acquired first may lead to an explanation of this occurrence. There may be a direct relationship between the spatial and temporal concepts that the child is capable of dealing with at this stage of development, and the early selection of the members of a class for use in sentences. Not only are there some members of a class which are acquired before others but there is a period of time in which these first acquisitions are substituted for each other in sentences. These substitutions may be the result of nonobservation of the complete set of properties of a lexical item in some instances (that is, incomplete dictionary entries) which is caused by incomplete differentiation of members of a class. In many other instances, these substitutions seem to be the result of nonobservation of the contextual constraints imposed by syntactic rules on cooccurrence of different members of different classes. These are instances of both incomplete semantic and syntactic rules. Finally, during this age period, the child uses the members of a class redundantly to ensure syntactic correctness or to ensure that meaning is conveyed completely. He also uses the members of a class conjointly to express a meaning for which he has not yet acquired a lexical item.

2.4 Morphological Rules and Phonology

We have chosen to discuss morphological rules at this point because the trends we observe with the use of these rules is very analogous to those we have already observed in the use of base structure rules. We have noted developmental trends in inflectional rules for person, number, tense, and possessives. We have not analyzed the data to look for developmental trends in the use of prefixes and suffixes and the various grammatical roles they play. The understanding and use of morphological rules is potentially a very rich area for examination by experimental means, and has already been treated experimentally to some extent.[29]

As in the case of base structure rules where all the children could generate all the basic syntactic classes in various contexts, all the children in this population could apply the grammatical markers of person, number, tense, and possessives in various restrictive contexts. At the same time, they would, on occasion, not apply the grammatical markers or apply them in conflict with selectional restrictions or apply them once more after they had already been applied appropriately. We again observe cases of (1) nonexpansion of a symbol in the string, (2) conflict with selectional restrictions, and (3) further expansion of a terminal symbol.

There are two aspects of morphological rules which often confuse the issue of whether or not the child has already acquired the rule or not. Application of a morphological rule is dependent on phonological context. For example, with the morpheme 'boot' the plural is marked by + *s* while with the morpheme 'hood' the plural is marked by + *z*. Past tense forms are also restricted by phonological context. In addition to this aspect, there are, developmentally, some sounds which are presumably mastered at a later time than others. Among these are the sibilants *s* and *z*. The question of whether or not the child understands singular and plural markers, present and past tense markers, possessive markers, and cases of Pronouns is not completely answered by the types of deviations that are observed. This is especially true of the age range we are now discussing where deviations are the exception rather than the rule. We cannot state that because a child produces the plural of 'house' as 'house' that he doesn't understand the rule of pluralization or observe it because he also produces 'books,' chairs,' 'crayons,' etc. There may be some specific aspect of 'house' such as its final *s* sound which leads him to this result. When he produces the plural of 'house' as 'housiz' rather than 'houziz' we can state that he doesn't know the rule of voicing the final unvoiced consonant in certain contexts (+ strident) before adding the plural marker. We can especially state this when we observe that he produces 'wolfs,' and 'bathiz' as well. However, we cannot state that he doesn't understand that Nouns can be singular or plural and must be so marked. We can simply state that certain generalizations are being made about morphological rules and note what these generalizations are and in which contexts they are made. Of course, frequently the context in which generalizations occur is in the case of the irregular or strong form of Nouns and Verbs, but generalizations also occur with regular forms. Another source of generalization is the mass Noun but not as frequently, even in the youngest age group, as one might imagine.

Nonexpansion of a grammatical marker, or omission, takes place in the following contexts:

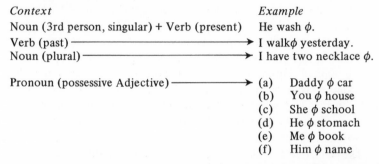

Context	*Example*
Noun (3rd person, singular) + Verb (present)	He wash ϕ.
Verb (past) ⟶	I walkϕ yesterday.
Noun (plural) ⟶	I have two necklace ϕ.
Pronoun (possessive Adjective) ⟶	(a) Daddy ϕ car
	(b) You ϕ house
	(c) She ϕ school
	(d) He ϕ stomach
	(e) Me ϕ book
	(f) Him ϕ name

Several observations should be made about these deviations. One should note first that in instances of Verb tense and pluralization of the Noun the context marks the fact that the marker has not been applied: He + Verb, Verb + yesterday, and two + N. There may be instances in which markers are not applied that we are not aware of because context does not clearly mark the deviancy (I walk? a lot, I have? red toy?). Berko's study[29] circumvented this problem by asking the child to make the appropriate choice of marker in specific contexts and apply them to a nonsense stem. The children in the study had already acquired the morphological rules examined. One would like to take the question one step further back and remove it entirely from the phonological context of the specific language. That is, mark, for example, pluralization in a manner different from English ('roog, roogi' versus mik, mikae,' etc.) and note the order of acquisition of markers (plural versus tense) and the generalizations made depending on the complexity of the system designed.

All of the occurrences of ϕ in third person, singular, present took place in this language sample when the Noun was expanded as a Pronoun (syntactic rule) and the Verb ended in an unvoiced consonant (a phonological rule). It may be a random occurrence, or one or the other or both of the contextual rules might be in operation. The influence of contexts might be teased out by observing in which contexts omission is accepted and in which it is not, if any.

The possessive form is presumably derived from a transformational rule which converts the X_1 of X_2 into X_2's X_1. What seems to be occurring in

cases a-d above is that the conversion takes place without application of
the possessive marker. That is, 'the book of Billy' becomes 'Billy book'
and 'the house of you' becomes 'you house.' In cases e and f it may be
that Noun, when expanded into Pronoun, always goes to the marked
Pronoun. The above rule is then applied in a similar manner ('the book of
me' becomes 'me book'). This seems unlikely since the children who produce these possessive forms do not also produce sentences such as "Me go"
and "Him stay," etc. An alternative explanation has to do with phonological similarity. We do not find instances of 'I toy' but only "Me toy."
'Me' is more like 'my,' and 'him' is more like 'his.' The generalization rule
which may be in operation in these instances is not clear since the occurrence of this form is infrequent and therefore, opportunity for systematic
analysis is limited. Again, this aspect of morphological rules should be
further explored by a systematic examination of preference of form (I toy,
me toy, my toy; he book, him book, his book). Note that in the case of
the feminine Pronoun, the marked Pronoun is the appropriate form in the
possessive case (her school).

The irregular or strong Nouns and Verbs account for the major portion
of deviancies observed. Taking the four Verbs 'be,' have,' 'go' and 'do' all
the following deviations are observed in nonapplication of a morphological
rule:

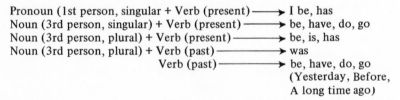

Pronoun (1st person, singular + Verb (present) ——→ I be, has
Noun (3rd person, singular) + Verb (present) ——→ be, have, do, go
Noun (3rd person, plural) + Verb (present) ——→ be, is, has
Noun (3rd person, plural) + Verb (past) ——→ was
                      Verb (past) ——→ be, have, do, go
                                        (Yesterday, Before,
                                        A long time ago)

In the case of strong Nouns when the plural marker is not applied the form
is that of the singular (a lot of child ϕ, many man ϕ, etc.).

Conflict with selectional features (or substitution) usually takes place in
the context of strong forms of Nouns and Verbs. The singular form of the
Noun is substituted for the plural plus the addition of the plural marker,
the present stem of the Verb is substituted for the past plus the addition
of the regular past marker, and the possessive marker ('s) is attached to the
possessive Adjective being used.

Noun (plural) ——————→ mans, childs
                      wolfs, housiz, bathiz
Verb (past) ——————→ comed, breaked, catched
Possessive ——————→ youz, hez, himz, mez

Attaching the third person, singular to the untransformed stem occurs with the Verbs 'be,' 'have' and 'do,' particularly in the youngest age group.

Verb (present) ⎯⎯⎯⎯→ bez, dooz, havez

Further application of a grammatical marker after it has already been appropriately applied, or redundancy, takes place with both strong and weak forms, although much more frequently with the strong forms.

Noun (3rd person, singular) + Verb (present)⎯→putsiz, doesiz, goesiz hasiz
Verb (past) ⎯⎯⎯⎯⎯→ liketed, splashted, camed
Noun (plural) ⎯⎯⎯⎯→ friendsiz, trainsiz, mouthsiz,
                         childrens, peopleses
Noun (mass) ⎯⎯⎯⎯→ milks, soaps, furnitures
Possessive ⎯⎯⎯⎯⎯→ Billy'siz

In the last two types of rules (substitutions and redundancy) one can clearly observe generalizations of rules taking place. It is obvious that the child wishes to apply the appropriate marker and can do so but cannot observe the restrictions on morphological change of stems of usually strong forms of Nouns, and Verbs, before those markers can be applied. For the most part these changes must be stored in memory as a list and therefore require a longer time for their mastery than do systematic changes governed by rules. An example of this is that although forms such as 'wolves' appear after forms such as 'muffs,' they appear before many of the plural forms of strong Nouns. The rules governing changes such as 'wolf' to 'wolves' apply to a small subset of the Nouns, but they, nevertheless, apply to a set, rather than each morpheme being a unique instance as is the case with irregular or strong morphemes.

The plural marker being added to mass Nouns takes place only when the mass Noun is an object and is being modified by Quantifiers. (some, a lot of, or lots of, many). "I want some milks" and "I have a lot of soaps" is found but not 'The milks is there' or 'I want the milks.' The explanation for this restrictive occurrence may be that when the mass Noun is Subject one can observe that the singular form of the Verb is always used. Also, the Quantifier usually modifies a plural Noun. We say "I want some apples," "I see lots of shoes," and "I took many books," but not 'apple,' 'shoe,' and 'book' in these contexts. The child is probably observing at least two aspects of contextual relationships and deriving general rules based on his hypotheses about these observations. To achieve complete grammaticality he must put these rules together. A single rule must hold for all members of the class whether functioning as subject or object and whether they appear with Articles or Quantifiers.

The phonological contexts in which redundant markers for pluralization of Nouns and tense markers appear should be noted in the examples given.

In the context Noun (third person, singular) + Verb (present), often the Verbs end in a voiced strident and the plural Nouns also end in a voiced strident. We cannot account for this generalization merely in terms of the frequency of occurrence of Nouns and Verbs in these contexts ending in z to which iz is added. They do not occur that frequently. In the case of past tense markers of Verbs, the redundant past marker is always added in the context final /t/ (liketed, fixted, pushted, etc.). We do not know what phonological rules are in operation to produce these generalizations or if, indeed, these generalizations are governed by phonological rules rather than syntactic rules. We have tried to point out throughout the discussion that in some instances it is difficult to parcel out whether (1) past or plural marker goes to ϕ or if only specific phonological matrices are treated in this manner, and (2) past or plural marker goes to past + past and plural + plural or if only specific phonological matrices are treated in the above manner. The evidence seems to point to phonological generalizations rather than syntactic.

In Figure 2.2 the mean per cent of children in the three groups who are using the three categories of incomplete rules are plotted to indicate developmental trends. In the case of morphological rules omission or nonexpansion of the grammatical marker ranks highest for all three groups redundancy or further expansion of a grammatical marker ranks second, and substitution or conflict with selectional restrictions ranks last, except in the nursery school group where it ranks second. This would be the age period in which there is greatest growth in the acquisition of strong forms. The percentage of children using all these categories of deviant rules decreases over the age range.

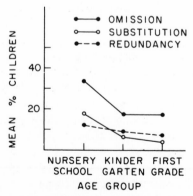

Figure 2.2 Mean percentage of children using rules with omissions, substitutions, and redundancies in morphological structures in nursery school, kindergarten, and first grade.

Table 2.3

Percentage of Children Using Single or Multiple Types of Deviant Rule within the Groups with Morphological Rules

Group	Single %	P Value	Multiple %
N.S.	34	.01	8
Kinder	21	.01	5
First Grade	16	.10	7

Table 2.4

Rank Order of Grammatical Markers used with Deviant Rules by Total Population and Each Group

R.O.	Total	% Type	N.S.	% Type	Kinder	% Type	First G.	% Type
1	Tense	56 O	Tense	77 O	Tense	44 O	Tense	46 O
2	Plural	34 O	Plural	45 O	Plural	35 O	Plural	23 O
3	Poss.	6 O	Poss.	16 O	Poss.	2 O	Poss.	0

We were again interested in determining what types of rules the children within the groups were using, as well as each group as a whole. In the nursery school and kindergarten groups a significantly larger per cent of the children were using one kind of deviant rule with a grammatical marker as compared to the per cent of children using a combination of types of rules with that grammatical marker. This was also true to some extent for the first grade children but less significantly so. These figures are given in Table 2.3. P values were obtained by χ^2 evaluation.

Deviant rules used in the application of markers for tense ranks highest for all three groups, and in all three groups, omission or nonexpansion of this grammatical marker is the type of deviant rule used by the greatest percentage of children. It should be noted that these numbers include those children who do not observe the person and number of the Noun dominating the Verb when applying tense markers for both strong and weak Verbs. The rank order of forms with the percentage of children using deviant rules with these forms is given in Table 2.4. As in Table 2.2, the letter beside each per cent indicates the type of deviant rule used by the greatest percentage of children in each group.

Again, these figures are a lumping together of many aspects of morphological rules, and certain aspects of morphology, as has been indicated, have been omitted entirely. Prefixes and suffixes, comparatives and superlatives and derived Adverbs (ending in *ly*) have been ignored and are potentially a rich source for determining the kinds of generalizations children make about the linguistic data. In the last category, a glance through the data would lead one to believe that the most frequent occurrence of a deviant rule is omission of the ending ("real pretty," "awful big," "real too little," "jumped quick," etc.), but generalizations such as "I'll draw that straightly" do occur. We would like to determine, for example, if there are any rules of cooccurrence in terms of both properties of Adverbs and Adverb placement which govern these deviancies. We say "I'll quickly draw that" and "I'll draw that quickly," but not "I'll straight draw that."

The figures computed and drawn are, also, a lumping together of many aspects of the morphological rules which have been discussed. For example, looking at the sentences produced by nursery school children one notes the frequency of occurrence of forms such as: I, you, he, we, they, you "be," all of which have been classified as omission of tense marker. On the other hand, the most frequent form of omission of tense marker in the first grade group is the following: "eyes is," "names is," "animals is," "momma and poppa is," etc. There is a striking degree of grammatical development which is not measured by these classifications. One would hope for much more insightful means of establishing the presence or absence of grammatical markers in the grammar than just observation before more qualitative measures are attempted. Those of us who are interested in the effect of memory capacity on language acquisition would be especially interested in the rate of acquisition of appropriate forms of strong Verbs and Nouns by children.

Another factor is that as the more elaborated forms of sentences are used, the more the rules that have to be observed. That is, there are more symbols in the string to expand and there are more selectional restrictions on cooccurrence of feature symbols in the string. The categorizations that have been made do not take into account this factor. They, nevertheless, give us some notion of the kinds of rules children use to generate their sentences at various stages of development during this age range.

Notes

1. N. Chomsky, *Aspects of the Theory of Syntax* (Cambridge, Mass.: The M.I.T. Press, 1965).

2. The T element indicated has been described as Pre Sentence

$$\rightarrow \begin{pmatrix} Q \\ Imp \end{pmatrix} \qquad (Emp) \qquad (Neg)$$

3. Each dictionary entry is marked in terms of its semantic and syntactic properties. It has been suggested that syntactic properties should be those concerned with

agreement between items in the string and semantic properties those concerned with definition. What should be marked as syntactic or semantic properties remains a question.

4. Phonetic symbols are used to represent a bundle of features such as −vocalic
   +consonantal
   +voice, as described in M. Halle, "On the role of simplicity in linguistic descriptions," American Mathematical Society, *Proceedings of Symposia in Applied Mathematics: Structure of Language and Its Mathematical Aspects, 12,* 89-94 (1961).

5. See J. I. Murai, "Speech development of infants," *Psychologia III,* No. 1, 29-35, (1960); D. McCarthy, "Language development in children." In L. Carmichael, ed., *Manual of Child Psychology* (New York: Wiley, 1954), pp. 492-630.

6. P. Lieberman, *Intonation, Perception, and Language* (Cambridge, Mass.: The M.I.T. Press, 1967).

7. The term "topic" is taken from J. Gruber, "Topicalization in child language," Mimeo, Cambridge, Mass.: M.I.T. Modern Languages Dept., March, 1966.

8. B. Z. Friedlander, "The effect of speaker identity, inflection, vocabulary, and message redundancy on infants' selection of vocal reinforcers." Paper presented at Society for Research in Child Development, Biennial Meeting, March, 1967.

9. None of the morphemes were produced accurately at this stage. For example, 'light' was produced as 'igh,' 'bottle' as 'batu' and 'car' as 'ta.'

10. P. Menyuk, "The role of distinctive features in children's acquisition of phonology," *J. Speech Hearing Research, 11,* 138-146 (1968).

11. For example, M. D. S. Braine, "The ontogeny of English phrase structure," *Language, 39,* 1-13 (1963).

12. D. McNeill, "Developmental psycholinguistics." In F. Smith and G. A. Miller, eds., *The Genesis of Language* (Cambridge, Mass.: The M.I.T. Press, 1966).

13. Ruth Weir, *Language in the Crib* (The Hague: Mouton and Co., 1962).

14. U. Bellugi and R. Brown, eds., *The Acquisition of Language* (Lafayette, Ind.: Monographs of the Society for Research in Child Development, No. 29, 1964). The Brown and Frazer paper (pp. 43-79) and the Miller and Ervin paper (pp. 9-35) contain exemplars.

15. Gruber presents an argument for describing these early utterances as "Topic-Comment" constructions. (J. Gruber, "Topicalization in child language," Mimeo, M.I.T. Modern Languages Dept., March, 1966). Although the "Topic-Comment" construction does not exist in English it does exist in other languages and the Subject-Predicate construction, according to Gruber, may be considered to be a special case of the "Topic-Comment" construction.

16. John H. Flavell, *The Developmental Psychology of Jean Piaget* (New York: Van Nostrand, 1963), pp. 122-163.

17. P. Lieberman, *Intonation, Perception, and Language* (Cambridge, Mass.: The M.I.T. Press, 1967).

18. In the use of Adjective one can say 'The happy, intelligent, handsome boy' but not 'The purple, intelligent, handsome boy,' and in the use of conjunction one can say 'I see a brush, comb, and nail polish' but not 'I see a brush, comb, and love.'

19. J. H. Greenberg, "Some universals of grammar with particular reference to the order of meaningful elements." In J. H. Greenberg, ed., *Universals of Language* (Cambridge, Mass.: The M.I.T. Press, 1963), pp. 58-85.

20. Omission of the Subject Noun Phrase only occurs in the context Pronoun, first person singular. Omission of the Object Noun Phrase only occurs in the context Adjective + Noun.

21. Omission of the main Verb of the Verb Phrase only occurs in the context Copula + Predicate Nominal or Adjective.

22. Nonobservation of differentiation of the form of Pronoun Subject and Pronoun

Object in such sentences as "Me a good boy" and "Him did it" are not appropriately classified under this discussion. It has been noted that this nondifferentiation of form may be due to the child's classification of the marked Pronoun as Noun in his grammar. See J. Gruber, "Topicalization in child language," Mimeo, Cambridge, Mass.: M.I.T. Modern Languages Dept., March, 1966.

23. The active-passive differentiation in the use of 'have' and certain nouns is not being observed. We say 'He has a cold' but not 'He takes a cold.'

24. Note, however, that it is permissible to say 'does the dishes.' The Verb 'does' is used very frequently in a general manner by children to express work of some kind as in the sentence "She does coloring."

25. In the case of Prepositional Phrases of time, the duration in time of the Noun Phrase of the Prepositional Phrase seems to dominate the Preposition. In the case of the Prepositional Phrases of location, the properties of the Noun Phrase in the Prepositional Phrase or of the Object may dominate the Preposition. (We say "stay at the hotel" but not 'at the puppy' or "He took a ride at . . ." but not 'He took me at . . . .'). In other instances the properties of the main Verb + Object may dominate the Preposition. (We say "He's pointing to it" but not 'He's pointing X to it.')

26. After the *separation* transformation has been applied this sentence is derived.

27. Ferdinand de Saussure, *Course in General Linguistics*, C. Baily and A. Sechehaye, eds. (New York: Philosophical Library, 1959).

28. T. A. Musseyibova, "The development of an understanding of spatial relations and their reflection in the language of children of preschool age." In B. G. Anan'yev and B. F. Lomov, eds., *Problem of Spatial Perception and Spatial Concepts* (Washington, D.C.: NASA, NASA Technical Translation, June, 1964).

29. Jean Berko, "The child's learning of English morphology," *Word, 14,* 150-177 (1958).

3 Transformational Structures in Sentences

Elementary transformations consist of a sequence of operations such as addition, deletion, permutation, and substitution. These operations effect changes on underlying base structure strings. In this way various sentence types are derived. Generalized transformations operate on a set of underlying strings (always at least two) to produce a single derived string. With the operations of embedding and conjunction, sentences that are indefinitely long can be generated.[1] Transformations can be cyclic (that is, reapplied to derived strings to create different derived strings) and they can be conjunctively and disjunctively ordered.

Linguistic theory postulates that the order of use of rules in the generation of utterances is first the formulation of base structure rules which contain semantic, syntactic, and phonological features. Within the base structure string are elements which indicate the transformations that are either applicable or obligatory. The string then goes through a transformational filter from which the surface structure of the string is derived. The derived surface structure is then acted upon by phonological rules to generate the utterance. The function of transformational operations, then, is to change base structure strings into various forms to which phonological rules can apply.

3.1 Simple Transformations

It has been held that the child first acquires some base structure rules and then some transformational rules.[2] It can be presumed, of course, that, in addition to base structure syntactic rules, some semantic properties of lexical items have been acquired, and that either some phonological properties and rules or some phonetic sequences related to a bundle of semantic properties have been acquired, since the child does communicate meaningfully at this 'pretransformational' stage of development.

An argument has been presented for assuming that the structure of the simple-active-declarative sentence is the underlying structure of the sentences the child uses during this period. To this basic sentence, the child, at some later stage, presumably applies transformational rules.[3] Observations have shown that children do not speak well-formed simple-active-declarative sentences first and then other sentence types, nor do they presumably hear them with any great frequency.[4]

In a formal description, the active-declarative sentence need not be any less complex than a negative or question sentence. Differences in descriptive complexity are due to the complete underlying structure of a string. Therefore, in some instances, an active-declarative utterance may be 'more complex' than, for example, a negative sentence. However, there have been experiments which indicate that in the case of utterances that have the same deep structure except for differences in the application of transformational rules, adult subjects more easily recall the active-declarative form of a string than the negative, question, or passive form of the same string.[5] The results are not completely consistent with the hypothesis that increasing the number of transformational operations applied to a string increases the difficulty in recalling the string. For example, N P Q (negative, passive, question) sentences are more frequently correctly recalled than Q P sentences. However, as was noted earlier, one cannot, with any confidence, ascribe the behavior of the adult to the child.

It is possible that one can describe a pretransformational period in the child's acquisition of language although it is inaccurate to state that children's first sentences can be described as simple-active-declarative sentences versus negative or question sentences. There may be a period in which the child is, indeed, generating his utterances with certain base component rules alone and that it is only at some later stage of development that transformational rules are applied. It is also possible that it is only at a still later stage of development that sentences are produced which are a combination of sentence types (N Q).

There is certainly sufficient evidence to indicate that early forms of sentences cannot be described as being generated by the same rules and the same order of application of rules as postulated for the completely grammatical derivation of various sentence types.[6] If we examine the sentence types that are being produced by children after the period of sentence-like words we observe that declaratives, question, negative, and imperative sentences are being produced. However, if the observations that have been made are accurate, the child is also producing these four sentence types in the earlier period.[7] It was noted in the discussion of base component rules that the underlying structure of early utterances may include an intonational marker (declarative, emphatic, and question) which is used generatively. Negative sentences may, at this stage, consist only of the negative morpheme "no."

As has been indicated, there is no hard evidence that intonational markers are being used generatively during the earliest period of 'sentence' production, but in the somewhat later period there is ample evidence that this is the case. In an exchange between a mother and child (age 2,0) the following utterances were produced:

1. C – Where Uncle Nat?
   M – (No reply)
2. C – Uncle Nat, Sylvia uh school.
   M – Sylvia's working.
3. C – Sylvia go to work?
   M – Yes.
4. C – and Daddy goes uh work.
   M – (No reply)
5. C – No goes uh work.

It is apparent that rules are being applied to change the structure of sentences. They either result in differences in the intonational contour (as in the contrast between sentences 2 and 3 or they result in the addition of a question or negative morpheme (as in the contrast between sentences 1 and 2 and between sentences 4 and 5). The question that has been raised is whether or not these should be considered transformational rules.[8] This question is critical in the opinion of some experimenters since if these utterances are nontransformational the child is formulating structural descriptions in his grammar for which he has no evidence (he hears transformed sentences), and these rules are highly abstract (found within the highest nodes of a sentence's tree structure). Therefore, one cannot postulate that acquisition of syntactic rules can be accomplished or, indeed, does take place, via a stimulus-response paradigm. On the other hand, exactly the same position can be maintained even if these utterances are produced with transformational rules since children do not hear sentences with the structures that they themselves use and the structures they do use can still be described as those within the highest nodes of a sentence's tree structure. Theoretically, it would seem logical to suppose that transformations are a part of the child's grammar in some form at the beginning stages of language acquisition since it is this aspect of the syntax which allows for the possibility of an infinite set of utterances and also allows for expressing different meanings using the same base structure rules (that is, 'Daddy goes to work' versus 'Daddy doesn't go to work').

Whether or not these early sentence types should be described as being derived from transformational operations on base structure strings or derived from base structure rules alone is a matter of theoretical opinion and one's definition of transformations. We can, however, observe developmental changes that occur in the structure of three of the sentence types produced at this stage: declarative, negative, and question. These changes seem to be due to the kinds of operations on strings that children seem capable of performing at different stages of development. There are no developmental changes that can be observed in the structure of imperative sentences per se. What does occur is that imperative sentences appear in the negative form ("Don't touch my crayons") and, to a much lesser extent, with tag questions ("Put that there, will you!"). Even with the tag question the utterance seems to be used to command rather than request.

During the earliest period in the formulation of these structures, the rules that may be used to obtain the various sentence types are of two kinds. The first, as has been noted, may be application of stress and intonational rules (., ?, !) on a single underlying string. The following are some examples:

Declarative: Shoe fall down.
                  Milks uh table.

Question: Mommy try it?
                  Diane uh school?

Imperative: Write on here!
                  Mommy try it!

At this stage the imperative sentence seems to have the following underlying structure:

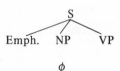

The above structure accounts for the imperative sentences in which NP appears and those in which it does not. The Pronoun class has not as yet been developed as a separate class in the language; therefore, it seems highly unlikely that these early imperatives are derived by deletion of the Pronoun 'you.' Further, at this stage, sentences which contain either the child's proper name as Subject and a Verb, or only the Verb plus Noun without a Subject, and without an emphatic marker ("Eric shake" and "Shake shoes") are often produced. The only structural difference between the Predicate constructions "shake shoes" and "shake shoes!" seems to be the application of stress.

The second kind of rule which may be used can and has been described in two ways. The rule can be described as (a) expansions of an element in the underlying strings (Q or Neg.) or as (b) the conjunction of an element or elements to derive a sentence type (Q, Neg., Decl.).[9]

a.

$$\left\{ \begin{matrix} \text{Neg.} \\ Q \end{matrix} \right\} \quad (NP) \quad (VP)$$

b.

$$\left\{ \begin{matrix} NP \\ \text{Neg.} \\ Q \end{matrix} \right\} \quad S^1 \quad NP \left\{ \begin{matrix} Pro \\ \phi \end{matrix} \right\} VP^{10}$$

Some examples are the following:

Declarative: Fix it, mommy's shoes.
              Read it, a paper.

Question: Where pencil?
              What you do?

Negative: No books in.
              No write dis.

It should be noted that question sentences with the Copula contraction appear also ("What's that?" and "Where's daddy?") but the much more frequent occurrence is the question morpheme without the Copula Verb ("Where pencil?"). Therefore, at this stage, the appearance of the Copula seems to be the result of memorization rather than generation. Also negatives appear in imperative sentences ("No touch!") and question sentences ("No pencils here?").

In the b type of construction there are restrictions of reference involved in the conjunction of the NP and S^1. For example, the word 'it' in "Fix it, mommy's shoes" refers to shoes. There seem to be restrictions on the conjunction of question morphemes and S^1 dependent on the VP of S^1. The child says "Where daddy go?" but *not* 'What daddy go?' or 'Who daddy go?'. There are many instances in which restrictions cannot be observed such as 'What's that?' 'Who's that?' or 'Where's that?' One cannot observe any restrictions on the conjunction of negative morphemes with S^1. They appear with Noun Phrases and Verb Phrases. One can only note that at the beginning stages of negative sentence development, a much larger number of these sentences contain the morpheme 'no' as compared to 'not.' This is interesting for only one reason. It may be a further indication that early sentence types are generated by the operation of conjoining elements rather than by an expansion of a node in the underlying strings. 'No' is an independent element, as are all the question morphemes, whereas the morpheme 'not' isn't independent. It is only when the negative morpheme is embedded in the sentence that 'not' begins to appear with any great frequency.

The first step in the acquisition of operations for the generation of various sentence types may then be conjunction of an element to a sentence with no operations on the underlying sentence but with some restrictions involved. In this way the sentence aspect of the underlying string is undisturbed and yet the child achieves greater definition in the expression of meaning. He cannot convey the contrast between negative and positive utterances when the negative morpheme is used alone ('No' and 'touch' versus 'No touch'), and he cannot convey the meaning of a specific question by the use of intonational markers ('Daddy go?' versus 'Where daddy go?' and 'Why daddy go?'). This greater definition, however, is accomplished without separating elements in the basic sentence. It is this operation that he cannot, as yet, perform on strings. Indeed, there is some evidence that the child doesn't understand WH Question utterances which involve inversion of the WH element and auxiliary Verb (the operations involved in the generation of a WH Question) nor negation utterances which involve attachment of the negative element to the auxiliary or modal (the operation involved in the generation of a negative sentence).[12]

Until the Auxiliary/Modal node of the categorial component of the base structure of the grammar is acquired by the child, completely well-formed structures cannot be derived and the transformational rules that have been described for the generation of negative and question sentences cannot be applied. When one observes independent use of Auxiliary/Modal one also observes completely well-formed negatives and questions. In the age period of 2,10 to 3,0 years the following types of sentences were obtained from children's language samples:

	Declarative	*Questions*
Copula	The snow is soft to me.	Isn't that funny?
Aux-be	My baby is eating.	Are there frogs swimming in there?
can	She can sit in my lap.	Can I see how he drives nicely?
do	I did read that motor boat book.	Do you remember me?
will	I'll hold it till you go home.	Will you go off again?

	Negative	*WH-morphemes*
Copula	It's not Amy's.	Where's my cabby?
Aux-be	I'm not going to fall off this horsie.	What's he doing?
can	Everybody can't have a turn.	Why can't I write on that?
do	I don't know that one.	How did he go?
will	You won't kick it down.	Who will help me?

In the early sentence types there seem to be only rules for conjunction of NP, negative morpheme, question morpheme, and sentence, outside of some base structure rules and prosodic features. Once the Auxiliary/Modal node of the categorial component of the base structure of the grammar is added, the transformational rules, as described, can be applied. At this stage, completely well-formed instances of the various structures Declarative, Negative, and Question, begin to occur much more frequently. There is a period of development between the two stages that have been described at which several types of structures can be observed.

In the development of question and negative sentences the following types of utterances can be observed.

Question

	WH-morpheme	*Copula*	*Auxiliary*
1.	Where (goes) the wheel (goes)?[13]	This powder?	Make it?
2.	Where the wheel do go?	This is powder.	He's make it?
3.	Where does the wheel goes?	Is this is the powder?[14]	Does he makes it?
4.	Where does the wheel go?	Is this the powder?	Is he making it?

Negation

	Modal	*Copula*	*Auxiliary*
1.	No do this.	No cowboy.	No touch.
2.	I no do this.	That not cowboy.	I not touch.
3.	I can't do this.	That's not a cowboy.	I'm not touching.

In the case of WH Questions, sentences 1 and 2 can be described as a conjunction of WH morpheme and a sentence, but in sentence 2 'do' appears. In sentence 3 'do' inversion has taken place but tense is marked both on 'do' and the main Verb. In sentence 4 the tense marker is applied appropriately. In the case of Aux/Modal inversion questions and Copula inversion questions, sentences 1 and 2 are produced by the application of an intonational marker, but in sentence 2 the Aux and Copula appear. In sentence 3 inversion of the Aux/Modal or Copula occurs but tense is marked on the 'do' support Verb and the main Verb, and thus is replication of the Copula. In sentence 4 tense is marked appropriately. The developmental steps that may occur in the generation of question sentences are as follows:

1. Conjunction of Q + S (or S with intonational marker)
2. Development of the Aux/Modal node
3. Q attraction   S $\longrightarrow$ $\begin{Bmatrix} \text{WH} + \text{that} \\ \text{WH} + \text{there} \end{Bmatrix}$ NP   Aux   VP
4. Inversion of Aux/Modal   S $\longrightarrow$ Q   Aux^{tense} NP   VP^{tense}[15]
5. Inversion of tense marker   S $\longrightarrow$ Q   Aux + tense   NP   VP

In negation sentences, sentence 1 can be described as a conjunction of the negative morpheme and a sentence. In sentence 2 subjects appear and the 'neg' element hops over the Subject. Sentences such as 'No I do this,' 'No (not) that cowboy,' and 'Not I touch' do not appear. In sentence 3 the Aux/Modal and Copula appear and either the 'neg' element is attached to the Aux/Modal and Copula or it appears between the Aux/Modal and Copula and the main Verb.

The steps that may occur in the generation of negation sentences are as follows:

1. Conjunction of Neg + S (Neg may appear alone, and S may be imperative.)
2. Development of Subject + Predicate sentences
3. Neg hopping   S $\longrightarrow$ NP   Neg   VP
4. Development of Aux/Modal node
5. Neg attachment   S $\longrightarrow$ NP   Aux+Neg   VP

It is obvious that not all children may proceed in the postulated step-by-step development. Also, there may be missing pieces in this described progression. Children may produce utterances during this period which indicate that there is a period in the development of negative sentences, similar to that observed in question sentences, during which Subject + 'neg' element are conjoined with a sentence containing Aux and modal before the 'neg' element is hopped (for example, 'I no can do this' and 'I not be touching'). There may be productions which indicate that, in both negation and question sentences, tense is attached only to the main Verb (for example 'he don't plays' and 'where do the wheel goes?'). Children may produce utterances which indicate that tense is attached to both the auxiliary and main Verb in negation as well as question ('He doesn't plays' as well as "Where does the wheel goes?'). In essence, there may be certain operations on base structure strings which children must be able to perform before they can proceed to the next operation, and, finally to the completely well-formed structure. The frequent longitudinal observation can indicate signposts in development. Observations of greater numbers of children at different ages may fill in details about possible progressions. Experimentation may reveal relationships between various stages of production and various stages of comprehension.

The major developments in the generation of various sentence types during this period seem to be (1) the conjoining of elements to sentences, (2) development of Subject + Predicate sentences, (3) expansion of the VP node to include Aux/Modal and Copula, (4) embedding an element within a sentence and attachment of the element to the Verb (either preceding as in the case of Q or following as in the case of Neg) (5) permutation of elements within the string (Aux/Modal and tense markers).

The grammatical operation of conjunction and the observation of some restrictions in the conjunction of elements is an important factor in sentence generation. It is a productive operation which the child will use with very great frequency, in an elaborated manner, at a later stage of development. Moving elements within the sentence is an operation which seems to appear later in the utterances children produce, and for a while the child maintains a contiguous relationship between the Q and 'Neg' elements and the Verb and between the main Verb and the tense marker. The operations involving separation of items in an underlying string to add, delete, or substitute other items is a more complicated task than conjoining items. Not only does this appear to be the case in these early sentence types but the same progression can be observed at a later stage of development when operations are being used on more than one sentence.

At the same time that children aged 2,10 to 3,0 years are producing completely well-formed declarative, negative, and question sentences, they and older children are producing not completely well-formed sentences. The following are some examples of question sentences. The age of the child producing the utterance is indicated on the left.

3,1   How you take it out?
3,3   What you are writing?
3,4   What's this plays?

3,5	What does this does?
3,9	Why you do with this?
4,0	Where Blacky is?
4,4	What they are doing?
4,8	How can he can look?
5,2	Where could be the shopping place?
5,4	Why they are here?
5,7	Where's going to be the school?
6,0	What's these things?
6,2	Where she's going?

The frequency of production of non-well-formed utterances decreases markedly, and the type of deviant rule that can be observed changes over the age range. However, it should be noted that throughout the age range there continue to be deviant utterances which are similar to those produced at an earlier age. A performance model must account for this fact and the changing structure of deviant utterances. This aspect of grammatical development will be discussed in the section on development of transformational rules.

3.2   Development of Transformational Rules

The basic transformations postulated as being present in the fully developed grammar are used by varying numbers of children throughout the age range during the period of 3 to 7 years. These transformational operations are applied to one underlying base structure string or two or more underlying base structure strings. The following are some examples without detail:

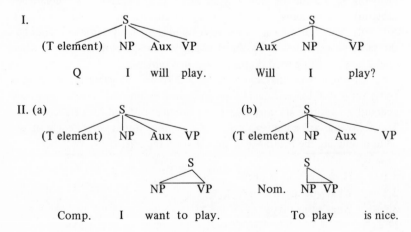

(c)

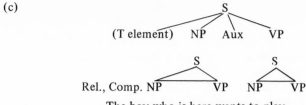

The boy who is here wants to play.

Type c may be considered to be an elaboration by using the rules of both a and b.

Unlike the completely well-formed base structure rules and morphological rules that have been described which were used by *all* the children in this population, it should be stressed that various transformational types were not used by all the children. The children also produced sentences which were approximations to completely well-formed sentence types. In most instances the children produced, simultaneously, completely grammatical exemplars of transformational types and approximations to these types. In a few instances there was a period during which only the approximations to the completely well-formed structure were produced. Then, during a later age, simultaneous productions occurred. These instances of only the approximation being produced occurred rarely during this age range. The few instances in which this occurred were:

Auxiliary Have ⟶ He been going to school.
He been thinking about that.

No instance of Pronoun + have, Contraction (I've been thinking about that) occurred, only the above.

'There' insertion ⟶ It isn't any more snow.
Now it's no more tail.

No instances of Pronoun + 'there' insertion occurred (There isn't any more snow), only the above.

In addition, some children did not observe an aspect of Adverb inversion. The restriction of observation of Verb number of the Verb 'be' in 'here' and 'there' inversions was always not observed by these children as in the utterances: "There's three trees" and "Here's the blades." Both the Auxiliary 'Have' and 'There' insertion transformations are used by a comparatively small percentage of children in this population (24 and 41 per cent, respectively), and a large increase in usage is not observed until the first grade period.

For the most part, then, more or less gross approximations to completely well-formed structures are produced by these children simultaneously with completely well-formed structures. The term 'more or less gross approximations' is used since at varying ages varying types of approximations occur with some transformational structures.

As with increasing grammatical sophistication in the use of base structure and morphological rules, the following observations can be made about the use of transformational rules: Children increase the number of varying types of structures that they use and increase the frequency of usage of these varying types of structures. They, also, increase the *elaborations* of these basic types of structures, and they gradually eliminate approximations to completely well-formed structures. Older children in this age range produced fewer types of structures with approximate rules, and older children produced sentences which could be described as containing closer approximations to completely well-formed structures than did younger children. As an increasingly mature population was observed and more varying types of structures were used by more children, there were periods during which the numbers of children using approximations to these more complex structures rose.

The following has been hypothesized about a model of perception: The perceiver acquires and stores the rules of a grammar. Using these rules and a heuristic component, the perceiver samples an input sentence and by a series of successive approximations determines which rules were used to generate this sentence. It has also been hypothesized that the perception processes for language are analogous to the production processes.[16] Therefore, it is possible that the transformationally deviant sentences produced by children in alternation with the completely well-formed structures represent more or less complete approximations to completed rules.[17] This does not mean that in the initial acquisition of a syntactic rule, we see a sequence of more and more complete series of rules used to generate a structure. Our information about initial acquisition is too incomplete and sparse to make such a definitive statement. There are some indications that this is not the case at all, and that initial rules are quite different in form from any level of derivation of a completely well-formed structure, as was discussed earlier. There is also some evidence contrary to the proposed hypothesis that adults perceive the underlying structure of sentences by internally reproducing their derivational history. They may, rather, be confirming some specific hypotheses about the relationship of the surface structure of a sentence and its underlying structure.[18] What is being indicated is simply that once the set of rules for the generation of a completely well-formed structure has been acquired the child sometimes *produces* what can be described as approximations to these complete sets.

We will explore grammatical development in the acquisition and use of transformational structures by discussing the types used by greater and greater numbers of children in this age range as one observes an increasingly mature population and the types of approximations to completely well-formed structures observed throughout the age range.

The possible development of some transformations according to data collected on early productions was traced earlier. It was noted then that in the earliest period of the age range we are now discussing the base structure rules, upon which transformational rules may be dependent, have been acquired. That is, the auxiliary node in the base structure string has been developed.

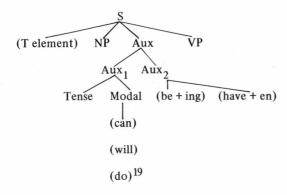

Previous to this development different kinds of sentences may be produced by the superposition of an element in the string (rising intonational contour, falling intonational contour, or emphasis), or by conjoining an item to the string in the case of negation and certain questions. Some restrictions on the placement of these elements are in operation even in the earliest sentences. For example, in the earliest stages of negation, utterances such as "no touch" and "not take mine" were being produced. However, at a later stage, when more complex forms were being produced, the addition of the negative element as the first item in the string was not maintained. Utterances such as 'No I pop on that one' and 'Not this buttoned' are not produced. Therefore, some observations about the placement of the negative element are being made even before the development of the auxiliary node.

When the auxiliary node has been developed the following three types of sentences can be generated using base structure and transformational rules:

Declarative
>He can + present go
>1 2   4   3

Permutation of the tense marker
1. He can go.

Negative
>He can + present not go
>1 2   4   5 3

Addition of element placed between modal and Verb
2. He can not go.

Contraction
>be ⟶ I'm, you're, he's . . .
>not ⟶ 'nt
>will ⟶ 'll
>He can + present + 'nt go
>1 2   4   5 3

Substitution of negative contracted element attached to verb
3. He can't go.

All of the children in this population produced sentences of the type 1, 2, and 3. The following kinds of derived structures are also produced by all of the children:

Auxiliary Be
>He be + ing go + present
>1 2 + 3 4 + 5

Permutation of tense markers
>He be + present go + ing
>1 2 + 5   4+ 3
>He is going.

Got
>I have + present a book
>1 2 + 3   4 + 5

Addition of Get + past tense marker
>I have + present get + past a book
>1 2 + 3   6 + 7 4 5

Contraction substitution
>I + ve get + past a book
>1 + 8 6 + 7 4   5
>I've got a book.

The restrictions involved in the 'got' transformation should be noted: have + present, get + past and contraction obligatory. This transformation is an alternate for the simple use of the Verb 'have,' but the transformation is used with much greater frequency than the simple employment of the Verb.[20] Deviant forms are frequently produced with this structure as noted overly often in the literature: "He gots," "He's gots," "He does got," and (most frequently of all) "I got." The first three examples seem to be direct substitutions of the Verb 'got' for the Verb 'have.' The last example, however, seems to be an alternate form of 'I've got' which is in fact used even more frequently than 'I got.' Alternation between the use of the contracted form of the auxiliary 'be' and omission of the contracted form also occurs with preschoolers under the age of 3,6. ("I going" and "I'm going.") However, in this age range, unlike the earlier age period, the auxiliary node is quite consistently being expanded indicating that it is an acquired class. At an earlier age auxiliary node expansion is in the process of being acquired and the contracted form of 'be' appears infrequently. There is a stage when the two forms ($\pm$Aux) are truly in alternation. At this stage it seems to be simply a matter of omission of contraction, or an omission of a rule in the derivation of the completely well-formed structure. Therefore, the occurrence of 'I got' seems to be another example of omission of contraction rather than Verb substitution and it occurs much more frequently than clear instances of the Verb substitution. It may be in fact that the Verb substitution takes place because of a generalization from omission of the contracted form of 'have.'

In contrast to the above two transformations which are used by 100 per cent of the children the full expansion of Aux_2 (be + ing have + en) is only used by 25 per cent of the children and by none of the children under age 4,0.

Auxiliary Have
  He be + ing have + en go + present
  1 2   3   4   +5 6 + 7
Permutation of tense markers
  He have + present be + en go + ing
  1   4   + 7   2 + 5 6 + 3
  He has been going.

As in the case of Auxiliary 'be' when the full expansion of Aux_2 is being acquired there are often occurrences of omission of the contracted form of Auxiliary 'have': "I been thinking about that," and "I been doing that." However, as we have stated, there are children who only produce the above forms and comparatively few of the children use the structure in its completely grammatical form. Therefore, unlike Aux 'be,' Aux 'have' seems to be in the process of being acquired by the children in the latter part of this age range.

We have given several instances of contraction both of the negative form 'not' and the auxiliary Verb. Contraction applies to modals as well. 'I'm, he's, (etc.), I've, he's, (etc.), I'll, he'll, (etc.)' can all be derived from application of contraction. When using these auxiliary forms plus negation, with Pronoun as Subject, there is an option to apply contraction to either the auxiliary or the negative element ('He isn't' or 'He's not'). What is involved in both contraction and negation is proper attachment of the added or substituted element. The contracted form of Auxiliary 'be' and 'have,' and modal 'will' (or the form 'would') is attached to Pronoun Subject. The negative element 'not' is immediately after the Auxiliary or modal or attached to it if contracted. In the earlier sentences various contracted forms are probably memorized alternate forms ('he' and 'he's,' 'I' and 'I'm') or memorized items ('can't' and 'don't'). They may however act as models for proper placement of contracted and negative elements. There seem to be some generalizations that children are making from this model to Adverb placement. Negation is not only indicated by the morpheme 'not' but also, for example, by the Adverb 'never,' the Nouns 'nothing' and 'nobody,' the Adjective 'no,' etc. There are rules governing the placement of these morphemes. The following deviancies might possibly stem from a generalization about the rules observed with negative morpheme placement:

Verb + Adverb

His mommy <u>is not back.</u>
His mommy is already back.
They follow around each other.
They lick all over him.
I like more to be with him.
I eat sometimes candy.
They play too with him.

Adverb + Verb

Mommy <u>never hits me.</u>
Mommy too makes candy.
They all together play.
They only are mad.

The contextual constraints of Adverb placement are not being observed in the above exemplars.

Double negation which looms very large in the ear of the hearer of children's language occurs infrequently in this population. The structure in most instances is the following example:

NP Aux + n't VP no NP   or   NP Aux + n't VP nothing
1   2 + 3   4 5 6   1   2 + 3   4   5
I don't want no milk.   I don't want nothing.

The generalization that seems to be occurring centers around the use of some, any, and no, and something, anything, and nothing, and their permissibility in certain contexts.[21] Context restrictions involve various transformations as in the following sentences where 'any' is not permissible in the declarative and imperative forms: 'You can put any water in it.' 'Put any water in it.' They also involve local selectional restrictions as in the following sentences where 'some' is not permissible: 'I don't know something about that.' 'He doesn't have some beard.' 'He doesn't get into some trouble.' The following sentences were actually produced as double negatives by the children: "I don't know nothing about that," "He doesn't have no beard," "He doesn't get into no trouble." It may be that 'no' and 'nothing' fulfill the requirements for both definite and indefinite properties of Adjectives and Nouns in children's grammar when there is some question about context restrictions, and represent the generalization of a rule.

The three derived structures Adjective, Nominal-Compound, and Possessive, are also used by all of the children in the population. They are related in underlying base structure and the operations involved in generating the derived structure. All are described as being derived from two underlying sentences one of which contains a Predicate Adjective or Prepositional Phrase with Copula construction or, in the case of Nominal-Compound, a Predicate Nominal construction.

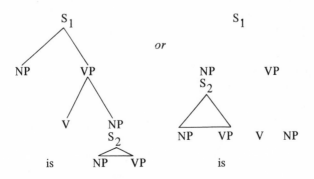

In generating the Adjective construction the restriction involved is that the NP of S_2 equal the dominating NP of S_1. In the following examples $3 = 4$ in deriving the first sentence and $1 = 4$ in deriving the second sentence. All of these constructions involve Deletion and in some instances Addition.

1st. S_1 NP   VP   NP
            1   2   3
            I want the book.

     S_2 NP   be   Pred. Adj.
            4   5   6   1 2   6   3
            The book is red $\longrightarrow$ I want the red book.[22]

2nd. S_1 NR   VP   Adv.
            1   2   3

     S_2 The book is there.
            NP   be   Pred. Adj.   6 1   2   3
            The book is red $\longrightarrow$ The red book is there.

It is perhaps because of the underlying structure of the derivation Adjectives, that is the restriction of Noun Phrase agreement, that the deletions we noted earlier, such as "I want the red," do not seem particularly deviant. The same is true in the case of the Possessive construction.

    S_1 NP   VP   NP
            1   2   3
            I am eating the cake.

    S_2 NP   Be   Prep. phrase
            4   5   6   1   2   6 + poss. 5
            The cake is of Joanna $\longrightarrow$ I am eating Joanna's cake.

The ellipse "I am eating Joanna's" also does not seem particularly deviant, possibly because of the same underlying structure as Adjective constructions.

Nominal Compound is described as being derived from the following types of underlying structure:

1st. S_1 NP   VP   NP
            1   2   3
             I   have   a monkey.

    S_2 NP   VP   NP
            4   5   6   1   2   6   3
            The monkey   is   a baby. $\longrightarrow$ I   have a baby monkey.

2nd. S_1 NP   VP   Adv.
　　　　　 1   2   3
　　　　 The carriage is here.

　 S_2 NP   Be   Prep. phrase
　　　　　 4   5   6   6   1   2   3
　　　　 The carriage is for baby ———→ The baby carriage is here

Although we do not find any deviant productions such as 'book red' or 'cake Joanna's' we do, with the youngest children in this population, find such deviations as "cow toy," "book motorboat," "car convertible." The fact that the Nominal Compound is derived from a combination of two Noun Phrases rather than predicate Adjective + Noun as in the case of the Adjective construction or Prepositional Phrase + Noun as in the case of Possessive probably accounts for the occurrence of this deviation. The ordering rules for NP, NP have not previously been established. For the same reason we cannot detect possible deletions with this construction as with Possessive and Adjective constructions where the fact that deletion has occurred is clear ('I want the red X.'). That reference is being made to an underlying NP is not clear if the second NP is deleted (I see the baby?).

Several other types of deletions which are completely grammatical are used by all the children in addition to the ones already noted. Some are derived from positive and negative constructions of modal + Verb:

NP   Modal   Verb
1   2   3   1   2
He   does   pay ———→ Deletion   He   does, etc
         can
         will

NP   Modal   + Neg. Verb
1   2   + 3   4   1   2+3
He   does   not pay ———→ Deletion He   does not
                     or   or
                     n't   doesn't

Others are permissible in the context of certain transitive verbs:

NP   V.   trans.   NP
1   2   3   1   2
He   eats   something ———→ Deletion He   eats

The one other construction used by all the children in this population is the infinitival complement:

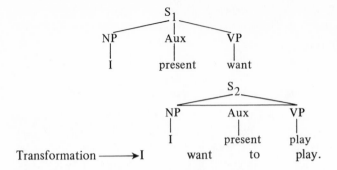

Transformation ⟶ I   want   to   play.

The operations involved in deriving this structure are deletion and substitution. There are restrictions on the permissibility of this transformation in terms of agreement between the NP of S_1 and S_2 and the properties of the Verb Phrase. We do not, for example, say 'I play to play' or 'I cut to play,' etc. In earlier sentences, constructions such as "I wanna" and "I'm gonna" frequently occur. These may be memorized items at that stage of development, rather than Complement constructions. At this stage of development we also frequently find "I wanna" and "I'm gonna." These, however, appear to be Complement constructions rather than memorized items for two reasons. First, the construction appears with additional Verbs such as "have to" or "need to" and "like to" or "hate to" and other types of Verbs in other types of constructions such as "I'm supposed to leave" and "I used to fall off." Second, the complement appears in sentences with Pronoun Objects such as "I want him to play," "She told me to sit down," "I teach him to jump." The restriction in these constructions is that the NP of the VP of S_1 = the NP of S_2.)

At the same time that all of the children in the population are using the Infinitival Complement less than half of them are using the Participial Complement (43 percent). About half of those using the structure are in the first grade (20 per cent). This structure is described as being derived in much the same way as the infinitival construction:

S_1	NP	V	NP						
	1	2	3						
	I	see	him						
S_2	NP	V	NP						
	4	5	6		1	2	3	5+pres. part.	6
He	licks	his tail ⟶			I see	him	licking		his tail.

There are a number of Verbs which can be used with the Infinitival Complement but not with the Participial Complement unless there is an object in S_1. These are Verbs which are used with great frequency, which may be a reason for the difference in usage of the two types of complements:

I have to play	but not	I have playing
I want to play	but not	I want playing
I need to play	but not	I need playing

Seemingly grammatical deletions occur with the Infinitival Complement both with and without an object in S_1: "I like to" and "I like him to." Again, in this transformation it is clear that a deletion has occurred ('I like him to X.') and that the deletion refers to a previously produced Verb. Other deletions concern the 'to' morpheme in the Infinitival Complement construction. Some of these are optional and others are obligatory. Both "Help me set the table" and "Help me to set the table" seem permissible and both types of construction appear in the language sample. In the sentences (1) 'He watches him put the paint on' and (2) 'He watches him to put the paint on' the second seems nongrammatical, although with the Participial Complement the sentence again seems grammatical, (3) 'He watches him putting the paint on.' Restrictions on the type of construction permissible are imposed by the properties of the Verbs used.[23] Sentences such as 2 never occur in the language sample and sentences such as 3 occur rarely. The rule is applied in only one way.

Along with seemingly permissible deletions, deletions of either the 'to' morpheme or the present participle ending of the Verb occur in these constructions:

We're going share.
I don't like tickle.
I like do it.
I want draw it.

Most of the above types of sentences are produced during the nursery school period. During the kindergarten and first grade period both the 'to' morpheme and the present participle ending may be employed in generating complement structures.

We've got to pasting.
Next year, I'd like to bowling.
She cooks and goes to shopping.[24]

These constructions are reminiscent of the redundant use of rules found in the base structure component of the grammar. Omissions and then, later, redundant use of rules is found with this structure as with base structure rules. Despite the fact that 100 per cent of the children are using the Infinitival Complement construction only 17 per cent are using the elaboration of this structure.

Iteration

S_1 You have comp you
    1   2   3   4

S_2 You clean clothes comp you
    5   6   7   8   9

S_3 You make them clean
    10 11 12 13

By deletion and substitution, with the restriction that subjects of S1, 2, and 3 are equal, the following sentence is derived:

  1   2   to+6   7   to+11 12 13
  You have   to clean   clothes to make them clean.

Some of the structures used by all of the children in this population have been discussed. They are not necessarily the simplest structures which could be produced, although it is true that in many instances these structures involve comparatively simpler operations (fewer in number) than those used by smaller numbers of children in the population. We have already cited some of these latter structures: Auxiliary 'Have,' which involves further expansion of the Verb Phrase; Participial Complement, which involves restrictions on usage with frequently used Verb types plus the attachment of the participle ending to the Verb; and Iteration, which involves expansion of a structure to an additional embedded sentence. However, simplicity, *in terms of derivational history,* is not the only factor in operation in the sequence observed in grammatical development. Structures which are used by all the children in the population, and which can be described as being derived from two underlying base structure strings rather than one, functionally operate in very much the same manner as previously acquired structures; namely Determiner and Object. They also serve the extremely useful function of increasing definition in communication. The Adjective types (Adjective, Possessives, and Nominal Compound) add a class of Determiners to modify Noun Phrases. Complement constructions increase the number and type of possible objects in a sentence ('I want a ball' and 'I want to go'). Therefore, the number of rules needed to derive a structure per se is not the only aspect of the grammar which determines which structures are used before others.

The utility of two other general classes of transformations used by all the children is obvious. Some form of the imperative and question were of course used by all the children in this age range. Questions were marked by generating declaratives with a rising inflection. "You didn't do that?" as they were at an earlier stage. In some instances the tag question was added, "She didn't spill on the floor, did she?" "He won't get dead, will he?" The *usual* form was negative statement + tag, rather than the inverse. Over 93 per cent of the children were using WH Questions and/or Aux/Modal inversion questions in the language sample obtained. The omission of standard imperative sentences in the language sample of some of the children is perhaps due to the linguistic style employed by the children in the particular stimulus situations. With the youngest children in the population (age 2,10 to 3,1) imperative sentences were used by all. A further analysis of the data showed that only 73 per cent of the children in the older nursery school population used the imperative sentences while 90 per cent of the children were using them in kindergarten and first grade. The older nursery school children were using forms of imperative other than deletion of 'you' sentences (Put the hat on! and Don't sit on my chair!) The following are some examples:

1. Would you sit down!
2. Please take this!
3. Let's make a dough cake!

The emphasis marker is used in all instances because although each sentence has an initial morpheme which would imply a declarative intonation or a question intonation they were produced in most instances as if they were the standard imperative. It is possible that the children were commanding, but in polite terms that had been acquired as alternative and "nicer" forms. Both the very frequent occurrence of 'could' and 'would' (rather than 'can' or 'will') and the frequent occurrence of negative statement + tag question, indicates that although the structure of the sentence is that of a question, children are, at this stage, frequently telling you rather than asking you.

In the discussion of earlier WH Questions and Aux-Modal inversions some of the deviant forms employed in the generation of these structures were noted. In summary, with WH Questions the following incompletions of sets of rules at various ages were noted:

a. Omission of modal

3,1　How you take it out?
3,9　Why you do with this?

b. Noninversion of Aux-Modal

3,3　What you are writing?

4,0   Where Blacky is?
5,4   Why they are here?
6,2   Where she's going?

c. Inversion of both Aux-Modal and main Verb

5,2   Where could be the shopping place?
6,1   Where's going to be the school?

d. Application of tense marker to Aux-Modal and main Verb

3,4   What's this plays?
3,5   What does this does?

e. Aux-Modal plus Aux-Modal/Verb

3,5   Is this is the powder?
4,4   How can he can look?
4,5   Is that's a belt?

The ages indicated and the types of sentences generated are merely exemplars of age range and types. Certain types of deviant forms occur early in the age range and disappear by the end of nursery school period (a, d, e). Others persist into the first grade period (b) and others only appear after the nursery school period (c). Possibly the e type of sentence is generated by the process of adding sentence to Noun Phrase, and therefore, is a reversion to a set of rules used at an earlier age to produce WH Questions. Another possibility, at this stage of development, is that a rule in these children's grammar for question sentence generation is reduplicate Aux in inverted position (i.e., *add Aux*) just as in the exemplars of the d type tense is marked in both main Verb and Aux-Modal. Type a sentences are produced most frequently in the early nursery school period during which nonexpansion of a kernel symbol occurs most frequently in general. Types b and c both involve rules for inversion in the generation of question structures. Type b, in which no inversion of Aux-Modal takes place, occurs earlier in the age range and type c, in which inversion of both the Aux-Modal and the main Verb takes place, occurs later in the age range. This type of process occurs quite frequently in the acquisition of a set of rules, that is, absence of an operation in generating a structure and then later overgeneralization of the operation.

In addition to the above types of transformational structures there are several others which are used by less than 100 per cent of the children in the population but are, nevertheless, used by a large percent of the children. Two structures are used by more than 90 per cent of the children:

(a) Adverb Inversion used by 97% and (b) 'and' conjunction used by 95 percent.

The Adverb Inversion structure takes two forms. With all Verbs except 'be,' only the Adverb or Prepositional Phrase are permuted to the beginning of the sentence in the following manner:

Adverb Inversion

NP	VP	Adv
1	2	3

I ride my bike in the afternoon.

Permutation

Adv.	NP	VP
3	1	2

In the afternoon I ride my bike.

When the Verb 'be' is used in this structure both the Adverb and the Verb are permuted as in the following examples:

There's a rock.
Here's a little house.
In the house is a bed.

Adverbs or Prepositional Phrases of place are most frequently permuted, and then Adverbs of time. No instance of permutation of an Adverb of manner ('Quickly, he ran') was found in the language sample. This is probably due to the fact that many more restrictions seem to be involved in permutation of adverbs of manner than the other types of adverbs. In these instances of Inversion with the Verb 'be' the restriction that Verb number remain the same is not always observed, and the following types of sentences are produced:

1. There's three lines.
2. Here's the blades.
3. In the woods was four dogs.

Sentences 1 and 2 might indicate that the 'There' and 'Here' inversions are simple Pronominalizations without any deeper analysis of the sentence, that is, NP, Copula, NP, but sentence 3 and the inversion of the Prepositional Phrase and Verb indicate that the analysis of sentences 1 and 2 is, Adv., 'be,' NP. The number marker is omitted as a feature of the Verb.

Conjunction with 'and' is used with increasingly greater frequency as an older and older population is observed. Some differentiation should be made between the sentence introductory 'and,' which has no dependent conjunction structure, and the transformational structure which imposes certain restrictions. The structure can be described as being generated by S1 + S2 . . . Sn, but not any S1 followed by 'and' any S2 such as "Blacky likes to pull the toy. And I have lots of toys to pull." This should be considered an instance of the sentence introductory 'and.' There are sequential and logical constraints on the conjunction of sentences. This is increasingly necessary in the use of other types of Conjunctions: 'But,' 'Because,' 'So,' and 'If.' Therefore, although the 'and' Conjunction is used with great frequency during the nursery school period the other types of conjunction are used by fewer of all the children in the total population and by more of the older children. 'Cause' Conjunctions are used by 82 per cent of the children (37 per cent are in the first grade), 'So' Conjunctions are used by 39 per cent of the children (19 per cent are in the first grade), and 'If' Conjunctions are used by 36 per cent of the children (20 percent in the first grade).

In all types of conjunction there are two structural restrictions that are in operation: Verb tense and Pronoun substitution. The following sentences seem deviant to us because these two types of restriction are not being observed:

John gets mad and she pushed the boy.
Bill falls in the lake so it got wet.
I'll hurt my brother if I scratched her.
My father never got sick because she catches cold.

The two sentences do not seem conjoined but simply strung together with a Conjunction morpheme.

In some instances of conjunction children do not observe tense restrictions ("He eats the cake cause he cooked it") and in other instances they do not observe Pronoun restrictions ("My baby brother has a gate cause she could fall down stairs"). No instances were found in which both tense and Pronoun restrictions were simultaneously not observed. At least one of the restrictions was always observed in every conjunction utterance.

In addition to these structural and sequential restrictions there are logical restrictions which are in operation. The following sentences seem deviant:

She is very good but very pretty.
I don't like cereal because I like eggs.

The dog is blindfolded so he got stuck with a knife.
If they put him in between he wants to go there.

As Vygotsky noted[25] there are instances in which a linguistic form is used before the child has acquired a full understanding of the meaning expressed in this form. We noted earlier, in the discussion of base structure rules, that there are instances in which lexical items are used without a complete knowledge of their properties. In the use of conjunction the functional relations expressed by the various conjunctive terms seem to be used before they are completely understood. A full and adequate description of these relations may belong in the semantic component of the grammatical rules. Just as cooccurrence restrictions mark sentences such as "The cow sings," as being deviant by semantic projective rules,[26] there are probably semantic projective rules which mark conjuncted sentences as being deviant because they violate rules of cooccurrence. No such description has, as yet, been written.

A possible explanation as to why 'cause' Conjunctions appear before 'so' and 'if' is that the direct and consequential relationships expressed in 'cause' Conjunctions are probably easier to acquire and understand than the conditional relationships expressed in 'so' and 'if' conjunctions, just as certain logical operations appear in the thinking of children before others.[27] This explanation, however, is admittedly gross. A description of the types of rules which are in operation in conjunction and a comparison between these rules and the rules in stages of logical thinking might be explanatory and mutually enlightening in terms of the observations that have been made about language and thought.

It should be noted that in the very earliest sentences various sentence types were formed by a conjoining procedure with some restrictions. The completely well-formed Conjunctions used at this stage of development require (1) a more elaborate set of restrictions which (2) carry over longer sequences requiring greater memory capacity.

Conjunction and Conjunction Deletion along with multiple branching rules create a possibility for indefinitely long sentences. Conjunction Deletion can take several forms. The form used by the children in this population is the following:

S_1	NP VP	NP	AND	S_2	NP VP	NP
	1 2	3	4		5 6	7
	I want the red crayon		and		I want the green crayon.	

Deletion

NP	VP	NP	AND	NP
1	2	3	4	7
I	want	the red crayon	and	the green crayon.

In this form the Subject and Verb are deleted and only the object of S2 is retained. This structure is used by 89 per cent of the children.

Another structure used by 89 per cent of the children is Separation with Verb + Particle constructions:

NP	Verb + part.		NP
1	2 +	3	4
He	put	on	his clothes.

Permutation

NP	Verb	NP	Part.
1	2	4	3
He	put his clothes on.		

The restriction involved in this transformation is that if the Object is a Pronoun the transformation is obligatory. Unless the Object is a Pronoun the string both before and after the transformation is completely well-formed ('He put on his clothes' and 'He put his clothes on'). This is not the case with Pronoun Object. Unless the transformation takes place the sentence is deviant ('He put on them'). In some instances the children omit a rule in the generation of this structure and do not observe this restriction. They produce utterances such as:

You pick up it.
He took out her.
Joanna took off them.
He beat up him.

These utterances occur with all third-person Pronouns both singular and plural but most frequently with the Pronoun 'it.' 'Pick up,' 'put on,' and 'take off' are the most frequently used Verb + particle forms found. This may be evidence that Verb + Particle constructions may be entered, *initially,* as a single entry. That is, both 'put' and 'put on' are dictionary entries.

The Relative Clause construction is the next most frequently used construction in this population (87 per cent of the children). The Relative Clause construction may be derived by substitution of the Noun Phrase of the Verb Phrase or the Noun Phrase of the sentence.

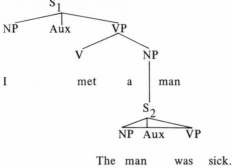

The restriction involved is that the object of S1 = the Subject of S2. By substitution rules and embedding the following sentence is derived: I met a man who was sick.

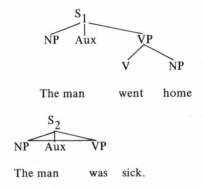

The restriction involved is that the Subject of S1 = the Subject of S2. By substitution rules and embedding, the following sentence is derived: 'The man who was sick went home.'

The 87 per cent of children using the Relative Clause construction are using the type I construction. Few of the children in the nursery school population are using the type II construction (six children), significantly more in the kindergarten group are using this type (eighteen children), and all of the children using the Relative Clause construction in first grade are using both types (forty-six children). Only 46 per cent of the children in the total population are using the second type of construction and 66 per cent of these are in the first grade. The reason for this difference in usage may stem from the fact that the precursor to completely well-formed structures derived from more than one underlying string seems to be simple addition. Before children are observing the set of restrictions involved in conjunction they are simply adding sentences together, observing the frame but not the content. In Relative Clause construction, for the most part during the nursery school period, a deviation observed is that sentences are derived with S1 + WH Question ('I know what is that') indicating that the Relative Clause is simply being generated in these instances by S1 + S2 rules rather than the rules described above. It is a generalization of the rule for conjunction. Further, there is no permutation in embedding involved in type I constructions. We have observed in other types of structures (WH Question and Negation, for example) that the operation of addition of a morpheme to derive the structure is used before permutation is observed. For these reasons the first type of completely well-formed Relative Clause to be used would be type I rather than type II.

It was noted above that there are restrictions of equality between the Noun Phrases of both sentences underlying the generation of the Relative Clause construction. There are, of course, restrictions involved in the form of the WH substitution for the Noun Phrase of S2. These restrictions also apply in WH Question sentences. No deviations from these restrictions are observed in question sentences such as 'What you do that,' 'Who you going,' etc. where the Verb Phrase seemed to dominate the NP and thus the choice of WH morpheme. In Relative Clause constructions, where the properties of the substituted NP dominate the choice of WH morpheme these deviations are observed. They are primarily use of 'what' for 'who,' 'which,' or 'that.' What is used for all the properties (human, concrete, animate, inanimate, etc.) of WH, in all instances, before differentiation has taken place. The following are some examples of nonobservation of restrictions on the WH form:

The boy whats crying is her brother.
I got everything what you got.
I see a dog what's white.

The very interesting question, still to be explored in both WH Question and Relative Clause is the ordering observed in the use of WH forms including Adverb substitutions ('where,' for place, 'how' for manner, 'when' for time).

One further observation can be made about the Relative Clause construction generated by the children in this population. It was extremely rare to find a sentence in which there was more than one Relative Clause structure ('I like the boy who goes to the school which is on the corner'). Although replication of structures were rarely found within a sentence (i.e., Relative Clause + Relative Clause or Infinitival Complement + Infinitival Complement) *varying* types of constructions were frequently found within a sentence, especially at the first grade level, such as, "I have a brother who goes to college to be a doctor." Sets of rules for different structures are applied to derived strings but rarely is the set of rules for the same structure applied to more than one string of the underlying structure.

More than 60 per cent of the children use the following two transformational structures. The Reflexive structure is used by 69 per cent of the children.

I cut I + self	We cut we + selves
1 2 3 + 4	
You cut you + self	You cut you + selves
He he	
She cut she + self	They cut they + selves
It it	

Substitution

NP	V	Pronoun, possessive + self (selves)
1	2	3 + 4

The restrictions are that Pronoun Subject = Pronoun Object (1 = 3) and that in third person the rule is:

NP	V	Pronoun, Object + self (selves)
1	2	3 + 4

By these rules the following forms are derived:

I cut myself.	We cut ourselves.
You cut your self.	You cut yourselves.
but	*but*
He cut himself.	They cut themselves.

In the case of 'she' and 'it' there is no morphological change from the possessive form to the object form that is necessary ('She cut herself' and 'It cut itself').

The restriction of Pronoun-Object substitution in the context of third person is frequently not observed so that both 'hisself' and 'theirselves' are often produced. In the case of 'she' and 'it' since there is no difference in form between Possessive and Object structures, we do not know if the restriction is being observed in these instances or not. In addition, the morphological rule of + pluralization in the context of . . . f + s ⟶ vz (as in the case of 'wolf,' 'wolves') is not always observed with this structure so that 'ourselfs,' 'yourselfs' and 'themselfs' or 'theirselfs' are all produced. Again, there is a generalization of a rule which can be noted in the deviant forms of this structure.

The Passive construction is used by 64 per cent of the children. The usual form of the Passive is the following example:

The boy present + hit   Jack
1   2   3   + 4   5

Addition and Permutation

He   present + 'be'   hit   by the boy
5   3   + 6   4   7   1   2

Deletion optional

He   is   hit
5   3+6   4

However, the *most frequent type* of Passive construction is the following:

He   present + *get*   hit
5   3   + 6   4
He   gets   hit.

We noted earlier the use of the Verb 'get' in the special and frequently used Verb form 'have got.' We see it being used again in the passive construction where 'get' is used in place of 'be.' It is also used for 'become' in Predicate Adjective constructions in the following manner:

He's becoming sick. ⎯⎯⎯→ He's getting sick.
He has become sick. ⎯⎯⎯→ He's gotten sick.

However, it is not used alone in Predicate Noun construction where it would seem deviant but it is used with 'be' in a Complement construction.

He's becoming a dope. ⎯⎯⎯→ He's getting to be a dope.
He's becoming a doctor. ⎯⎯⎯→ He's getting to be a doctor.

An infrequent deviation is noted in time Noun Phrases such as, "It's getting morning," "When it's getting nighttime . . ." These seem to be a direct generalization from Predicate Adjective constructions which involve time such as, "It's getting late."

It is possible that because of the uses of the Verb 'get' that it acts as an auxiliary along with 'have,' and 'be' and functions in place of 'become' in Copula constructions, in children's grammar, at least. However, this may also be true of adults' grammar as well where frequent alternate usage of 'be' and 'get' and 'become' and 'get' are also noted.

The two remaining structures which shall be discussed are a special instance of Pronominalization and Nominalization. The former is used by 41 per cent of the children and the latter by 29 per cent of the children. 'There' insertion in the context of a Noun Phrase with an indefinite Determiner takes place in the following manner:

'There' Insertion

NP	tense	be
1	2	3
No more	rain will be	

Addition and permutation

> There will be no more rain.

A frequent deviation is the use of 'it' in place of 'there':

It isn't any more to tell.
It was no more snow.
It's no more music.

This deviation probably stems from the fact that in the child's lexicon NP, general or indefinite (something) goes to 'it' as in "It's good for you." Also, in certain phrases 'it' always appears as in, "It's raining," "It's hot," etc. The context restrictions on the use of 'it' and 'there' are sometimes not observed by children.

The Nominalization constructions found in this population are (1) Objects, (2) Noun Phrases of Prepositional Phrases and (3) Adjectives. Type 1 constructions are described as being derived in the following manner:

S1	NP	V	Det.	N.
	1	2	3	4
	She	does	the	X
S2 ·	NP	VP		
	5	6		
	She	shops.		

Substitution and Embedding

NP	V	Det.	V + ing
1	2	3	6
She	does	the	shopping.

The restrictions to be observed are that the Subjects of S1 and S2 must be equal and that there are constraints on the cooccurrence of types of Verbs and Object Nominalizations so that sentences such as 'She plays the shopping' cannot occur.

Nominalizations can also be the Subjects of sentences as in 'Painting can be fun,' 'To eat frogs' legs is my greatest desire.' These types of structures are not found in the language sample of this population. Instead we find Infinitival Complement constructions such as 'I like to paint' and 'I like to eat frog's legs' and Object Nominalizations with Predicate Phrases such as "It's *good* to eat" and "It's *fun* to paint." The latter occur rarely in the language sample and are possibly memorized formulas since we do not find any sentences with any Noun Phrases other than the Pronoun 'it.' For example, sentences such as 'Ice cream is good to eat' are not found but only utterances such as "It's good to eat ice cream."

The second form of Nominalization found is Noun Phrases of Prepositional Phrases. The following are some examples:

He'll punish her by barking.
He'll stop them from doing that.
This is for braiding a rug.
It's to put powder on.
I dream about growing up and being an electrical.

This structure is described as being derived in the following manner:

S1	NP	VP	NP
	1	2	3
	He	'll punish her.	
S2	NP	VP	
	4	5	
	He	barks.	

Substitution Addition and Embedding

NP	VP	NP	Prep.	pres. part. + VP
1	2	3	6	5
He	'll punish her	by	barking.	

The same types of restrictions that occurred with Object Nominalizations occur with this type of Nominalization. There are several forms observed in the use of this construction:

1. That's for to brush your hair.
2. They won't help her baking a cake.
3. I dreamed about that I was going to school.

The deviation which occurs in sentence 1 is the type which occurs most frequently during the nursery school period, the type exemplified by sentence 2 occurs most frequently during the kindergarten period, and the type exemplified by sentence 3 occurs most frequently during the first grade period. During the earliest age period the problem seems to be to differentiate between the two forms ('to brush' and 'for brushing'). At a later stage the two forms have been differentiated and the important present participle form mastered, but the Preposition is sometimes omitted. At a still later stage alternate possibilities such as 'about' + Present Participle + Verb, and 'that' + S2, conflict in production. Restrictions on cooccurrence of types of rules are not observed.

The third form of Nominalization observed in this population is that of adjective. These are derived from underlying Relative Clauses in the following manner:

I hear somebody (who is) crying.
Look at the car (which is) crashing.
A farmer (who is) sleeping dead sees a cowboy (who is) riding a horse.

There are also forms in which permutation seems obligatory: 'Water (which is) boiling came'→ 'Boiling water came.' The most frequent form produced throughout the age range with Adjective Nominalization is the form in which the Nominalization modifies an animate object and appears as the last phrase of the sentence, as in "I see mommy tying a rope." Again, embedding at the end of a sentence, not requiring permutation, is the most frequent occurrence. The other forms of Adjective Nominalization (falling stars, jumping kids, etc.) appear more frequently at the older age level.

3.3 Transformational Operations

When we talked of the percentages of children using each type of transformational structure we lumped together several types within the category of this structure as in the case of the discussion of Nominalization. However, the overall trends give an indication of some of the processes that take place in grammatical development. Figure 3.1 indicates the rise in percentages of children using various transformational structures and the drop in percentages of children using deviant forms in the generation of these structures. The solid lines are straight lines drawn from age 2,10 to 7,1. The points indicate the actual percentages of children using these structures at each four-month age level between these two age points. There are no significant differences between the actual and predicted percentages at any age level.

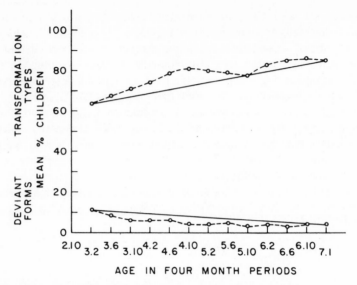

Figure 3.1 Mean percentage of children producing sentences involving the various transformations and deviant forms of transformations observed in the language sample at 4 months age periods.

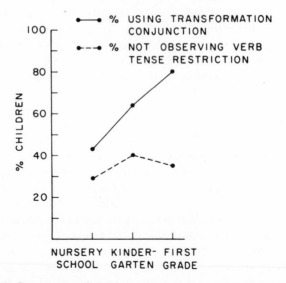

Figure 3.2 Percentage of children using all types of conjunction observed and percentage of children not observing Verb tense restriction in conjunction in nursery school, kindergarten, and first grade.

We can see some fluctuation occurring especially in the production of the deviant forms of transformational types. This fluctuation can be accounted for, in part, by the fact that increasing numbers of children are using increasing numbers of transformational structures as an increasingly older population is observed. As more children acquire a structure more of them are observed to use deviant forms of this structure as well as the completely well formed structure. As an example of this observation, in Figure 3.2 the percentage of children in nursery school, kindergarten, and first grade using several types of conjunction ('and,' 'because,' 'so,' and 'if') is shown and the percentage of children not observing Verb tense restrictions (the omission of a rule in conjunction structures) is also shown. During the kindergarten period the percentage of children using these structures rises sharply, and so does the percentage of children not observing Verb tense restrictions in conjunctions. However, by the first grade, although the percentage of children using these structures again rises sharply, the percentage observed to use the deviant forms of these structures drops, implying that this aspect of Conjunction derivation is being mastered for all Conjunction structures. Therefore, this fluctuation is due not only to increasing numbers of children using increasing numbers of structures but also to the level of mastery of the complete set of rules needed to derive these structures.

One aspect of grammatical development, then, as we stated previously, would be the use of more differing syntactic structures and decreased usage of approximations to completely well-formed structures as maturation takes place. This does indeed take place in this population. It has also been observed that this decreased usage of approximate forms is not asymptotic in nature but, rather, fluctuating, and cited the reason for this as being the effect of both the acquisition of more new structures and the level of mastery of these structures.

In addition to the above findings, that the sentences children use can be described as being generated by a greater variety of structures as they mature, it has also been found that there is a substantial increase in the numbers of children over this age range using structures which require operations on more than one underlying string. This is not the case with structures which require operations on only one underlying string. In the latter case there is very little change that occurs over the age range. These results are shown in Figure 3.3.

One other aspect of grammatical development is the production of closer and closer approximations to completely well-formed rules for the generation of particular structures as an increasingly older population is observed. Examples of this kind of behavior can be observed in the use of

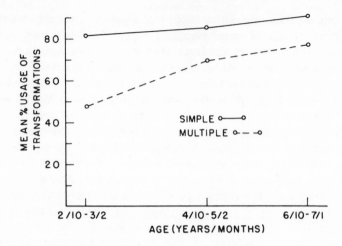

Figure 3.3 Mean percentage of children using transformations involving a single underlying string and multiple underlying strings at the beginning, middle, and end of the age range.

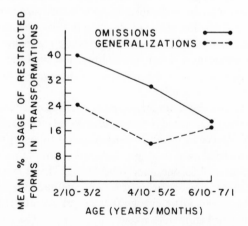

Figure 3.4 Mean percentage of children using omissions in transformational rules and generalizations about transformational rules at the beginning, middle, and end of the age range.

base structure rules, morphological rules, and transformational rules. We have cited instances throughout the discussion of transformations in which a rule or rules seem to be omitted in the generation of a structure and other instances in which a rule is being generalized. An example of this difference is the Verb Phrase Complement construction. In the early steps of development the 'to' is not produced in some instances ("We're going share"). At a later stage of development both 'to' and 'ing' appear in this structure ("We've got to pasting"). The number of children producing structures which can be described as having omissions of rules in their derivation drops over this age range but generalizations in the use of rules drop and then rise again at the end of the first grade period (see Figure 3.4). This rise is probably due to the fact that children during the first grade period are using many more structures than at an earlier period, and are not omitting but are generalizing rules in generating structures.

These are the quantitative facts that can be observed about the transformational structures that are used by children in their sentences. It would follow from linguistic descriptions of the grammar that there would be some operations on underlying sentences that the child would be able to perform before others to produce differing types of sentences. For example, he should be able to produce sentences with operations on single underlying sentences, such as negative, imperative, and question, before he can produce sentences which involve more than one underlying sentence such as embedding. In analyzing the sentences produced by children in this age range one finds increasing use of structures which involve more than one underlying sentence. It would also follow that, at the beginning stages of the acquisition of a structure, children should produce approximations to the completed structure based on previously acquired structures, and we find that they do.

Linguistic descriptions, therefore, not only describe the sentences children produce at various stages of development but also predict the course of developmental trends in language acquisition in terms of the structures that are produced earlier or later in the developmental course.

Theory might dictate that the more simple the derivational history of a structure (the fewer the operations needed to derive this structure) the more easily, and, therefore, the earlier it should be acquired. However, this, again, is only an *aspect* of grammatical development. It does not completely explain what we observe in children's linguistic behavior. Although, for the most part, sentences are generated from one underlying string before they are generated from more than one underlying string, the use of the Infinitival Complement appears to be acquired earlier in the age range by larger numbers of children than does, for example, the Reflexive or Passive, and is used by all of the children in the sample population, unlike the latter two transformational structures. In some instances the structural descriptions of certain classes are the same at some high level of categorization (that is, Determiner or Prepositional Phrase) but have properties which differentiate them from each other at another level. There are also constraints placed on their use by rules of cooccurrence in sentences which further differentiates them from each other. Dependent on the number of properties and type of properties (for example, definite versus indefinite Article; Prepositional Phrase of time versus place) and number and type of rules of cooccurrence, different members of the same class may be acquired at different times. We noted, also, that even with the same "type" of structure there are differences in time of acquisition. For example, Conjunctions with 'and,' including the syntactic restrictions on Verb tense and number and Pronoun substitution, appear early and are used frequently, but Conjunctions with 'if' and 'so' are used by much fewer numbers of children even late in the age range.

One further aspect of grammatical development was observed in the sentences produced at various ages by children. Certain structures not only appear before others but also are used with much greater frequency than are others. Completely well-formed structures involve certain types of operations. The terms 'deletion,' 'permutation,' 'addition,' 'substitution,' and 'embedding and nesting' have been used to describe these operations. Observing the order of structures produced by these children, from those produced by all to those produced by the least number of children in this population, and in terms of frequency of usage, the order of usage of operations seems to be as follows: addition, deletion, substitution, permutation, embedding, and nesting. This is far from an unqualified statement because of the interdependency of the other aspects of grammatical development that have been mentioned. For example, the use of the same operations does not guarantee that all structures which involve these operations are used at the same time and with the same frequency. The Infinitival Complement is used by all the children, but Iteration, involving the same operations as Infinitival Complement but with underlying S1, S2, S3, etc., rather than just S1 and S2, is used by only 17 per cent of the children. In the same manner, although conjunction is used by a great many of the children, the number of underlying sentences to which the operations of conjunction will be applied increases over the age range. On the other hand, it has been seen that structures which involve embedding of S2 at the end of S1 are used by many more of the children than structures which involve embedding at the beginning of sentences or nested constructions. Utterances such as, "I know the boy *who is sick*" "I need *to do that,*" "I like *that singing,*" occur more frequently than utterances such as *"What he did* was bad," *"To do that* is wrong," and *"The singing* is beautiful." These latter utterances occur much more frequently than utterances such as "The boy *who was sick* is back at school," "The reason *for doing that* is stupid," and "The dog *sleeping near the rock* is the brother."

To generate the sentence types (declarative, negative, imperative, and question) at an early age, the child uses operations which do not, initially, disturb the underlying sentence. It is only at some later stage that permutation of elements occurs within the underlying sentence. At a later stage of development, when the child is now dealing with embeddings of whole sentences, the same trend is observed. Again, his initial move is to add sentences to other sentences before disturbing the Noun Phrase-Verb Phrase relationship of underlying strings. He, therefore, adds before he deletes and deletes before he permutes in the generation of these sentences. It would be interesting to attempt to correlate observations of the order of acquisition of logical operations which are of a certain type and structure, and the order observed in the acquisition of linguistic operations, to see if some analogies could be found.

The observations about the limitations of the use of base structure rules and transformational rules in the sentences children produce indicate that grammatical development continues byond the first grade level observed in this study, at least in the production of sentences. However, the statement that all the basic syntactic structures postulated to be used by adults are used by the children in this population is correct. It is correct not only in terms of labeled structures, but also in terms of the syntactic classes and operations that can be described in the utterances they produce.

In the forthcoming chapter some studies which attempt to broach the question of children's grammatical capacity and competence at various stages of development more directly than does observation of language production will be discussed. One of the studies is concerned with a group of children whose language production has been labeled as being markedly deviant from the norm by other members of their linguistic community. In particular, the question of grammatical capacity will be examined in the light of the findings with this group of children.

Notes

1. J. J. Katz and P. M. Postal, *An Integrated Theory of Linguistic Descriptions* (Cambridge, Mass.: The M.I.T. Press, 1964), pp. 6-12.

2. D. McNeill, *Developmental Psycholinguistics*, Center for Cognitive Studies, Harvard University, 1965.

3. M. D. S. Braine, "On learning the grammatical order of words," *Psychol. Rev., 70*, 323-348 (1963).

4. T. G. Bever, J. A. Fodor, and W. Weksel, "On the acquisition of syntax: a critique of 'contextual generalization.' " *Psychol. Rev., 72*, 467-482 (1965).

5. J. Mehler, "Some effects of grammatical transformations on the recall of English sentences," *J. Verbal Learning Verbal Behavior, 2*, 346-351 (1963).

6. Comparisons may be made between postulated descriptions of children's sentence types and linguistic descriptions of completely well-formed sentence types. The claim that comparisons are being made between the rules postulated for children's productions and adult productions may be misleading since actual adult productions may also deviate from the postulated set of rules used to derive various sentence types.

7. During this period a large proportion of the utterances may be sentence-like words. However, it seems likely that two-morpheme utterances appear occasionally at this stage and that sentence-like words are used at a later stage.

8. A recent linguistic speculation has been that every kind of sentence type has a performative Verb. Roughly, declarative sentences such as 'The man hit the ball' are derived from the two sentences, S1—'I say to you' + S2—'The man hit the ball'; Imperative sentences such as 'Hit the ball!' from S1—'I command' + S2—'You will hit the ball'; and question sentences such as 'Will the man hit the ball?' from S1—'I request' + S2—'The man will hit the ball.' If this is indeed the case, then all sentence generation can be linguistically described as involving the transformational operations of embedding. How the performatives should be represented in a performance model of sentence generation (syntactically? semantically?) is an open question.

9. E. S. Klima and U. Bellugi, "Syntactic regularities in the speech of children." In J. Lyons and R. J. Wales, eds., *Psycholinguistics Papers* (Chicago: Aldine, 1966), pp. 183-219. The authors describe a structure of the type (a); J. Gruber, "Topicalization in child language," Mimeo, M.I.T. Modern Languages Dept., March, 1966. The author describes a structure of the type b.

10. The order in the b type of construction is free. S —→ NP (etc.) S^1 or S —→ S^1 NP (etc.). This would account for the appearance of the negative morpheme at the end of the utterance "Go to bed, no." No exemplars were found of the question morpheme at the end of the sentence such as 'Daddy, where?' It is possible that such sentences are generated by children.

11. Only this form of the declarative was found in the language sample. Other types were found by Gruber (1966) such as "It broken, wheels" and "Car, he take the wheel."

12. See E. S. Klima and U. Bellugi, Reference 9.

13. Utterances such as 'Where goes the wheel' and 'Where the wheel goes' both occur.

14. This replication of Verb or of tense marker occurs rarely in this question form, and is more usual in the declarative form. Utterances such as "He's goes there every day," "He be still be watching," "He's now is copying him," and "He's already's in the house" occur throughout the age range.

15. Tense does not seem, at this stage, to be an independent class. Therefore Verbs often appear alternately in their marked and unmarked forms (for example do/does and go/goes).

16. G. H. Matthews, "Analysis by synthesis of sentences of natural languages." (London: National Physical Laboratory, Symposium No. 13, 1961), pp. 531-543; M. Halle and K. Stevens, "Speech recognition: a model and a program for research," *I.R.E. Trans. Inform. Theory, IT-8* (1962); and G. A. Miller and N. Chomsky, "Finitary models of language users." In D. Luce, R. Bush, and E. Gallanter, eds.,

Handbook of Mathematical Psychology, Vol. II (New York: Wiley, 1963), pp. 419-492. See these sources for discussion of these hypotheses.

17. P. Menyuk, "Alternation of rules in children's grammar," *J. Verbal Learning Verbal Behavior, 3,* 480-488 (1964).

18. J. Fodor and M. Garrett, "Some reflections on competence and performance." In J. Lyons and R. J. Wales, eds., *Psycholinguistics Papers* (Chicago: Aldine, 1966), pp. 135-154.

19. There is some question about 'do.' Is it an expansion of the Aux node or introduced by transformational rule.

20. The use of the Verb 'got' will be discussed further in conjunction with Predicate and Passive constructions.

21. See P. Menyuk (Reference 17) for a discussion of this occurrence.

22. The position of the Article should be noted. There are rules that govern the order of Article and Adjective + Noun. No instances in which the order is not preserved are observed in this age range (for example 'I want red the book').

23. See P. S. Rosenberg, "Phrase structure principles of English complex sentence formation," *J. Linguistics, 3,* 103-118 (1967) for a description of restrictions of Verb categories in the use of Complement constructions.

24. The underlying structure may be Nominalization with the deletion of the determiner rather than a Complement construction (i.e., 'goes to the shopping').

25. L. S. Vygotsky, *Thought and Language.* (Cambridge, Mass.: The M.I.T. Press, 1962).

26. See J. J. Katz and J. A. Fodor, "The structure of semantic theory," *Language, 39,* 170-210 (1963) for a discussion of semantic rules.

27. Piaget has distinguished two kinds of relations between events, causal and implicative. Implicative relations are relations between mental states. In logic, A = B + B = C *implies* rather than causes A = C. See J. Flavell, *The Developmental Psychology of Jean Piaget* (Van Nostrand, 1963), Chap. 7. Implicative relations therefore may be observed by the child only after he has begun to observe causal relations.

4 Grammatical Competence

In the preceding chapter we discussed the information that can be obtained and the many questions that remain unanswered, after an analysis of language samples obtained either periodically from a small group of children over a period of months or years or from large groups of children at various ages in controlled stimulus situations. The question of determining which utterances, consisting of certain structures, are understood at various age levels, either according to the complete set of rules by which they are described to be generated, or in some other manner, is not answered by analyses of language production. The problem of determining which structures are memorized bits of language or are generated by certain rules in the child's grammar is not resolved solely by analyses of the language produced. As we stated, such analyses give us some idea of the parameters of this developmental process, the trends in this process, and possible areas for further exploration. Such analyses may also eliminate certain hypotheses about the method and content of grammar acquisition.

4.1 Testing Grammatical Competence

The problem of eliciting linguistic judgments from the child during the critical period of acquisition from birth to about 4 years is obvious and need not be belabored. This problem, has in fact, led linguists and psycholinguists to either ignoring this period or to relying on descriptive studies.

The value of descriptive studies, outside of providing some very much needed basic information about what *does occur* during a period of language development, is to indicate what we might possibly ask the child to make linguistic judgments about. This, of course, holds true for children older than 7 years as well as for the younger child. There are now hypotheses about reasonable, linguistically significant questions which can be put to the child, but the problem of how to ask these questions remains. As has been stated, we might turn to the techniques and tools that have been developed in the "language laboratory" to explore perception, discrimination, and identification of, and long- and short-term memory for linguistically significant classifications and operations and their application to unique linguistic contexts. These techniques can be applied to what have been observed to be possible responses from children at various stages of development.[1] Although these techniques and tools may not offer adequate explanations for the acquisition of language, they do offer means for exploring what is understood about language at various stages of development. Studies that have attempted this approach have been few in number.

The linguist's usual approach with native informants to determine the rules of his grammar is to obtain language samples and then to ask the informant whether or not certain grammatical contrasts that he has reconstructed from these samples are indeed significant in his language. The adult is asked this question directly. The child must be asked the question indirectly, but the same principles are involved. Several approaches to this problem have been employed and have shown themselves to be promising in reconstructing aspects of the grammatical competence of children at various stages of development. Others have yet to be attempted.[2] They include having the child identify grammatical contrasts in picture stimuli (for example, the Subject-Object relationship),[3] having the child (the older child, possibly beginning at the kindergarten age level) identify which is the correct structure in a contrast of two (for example, 'She going to the store' or 'She's going to the store') or the best in a contrast of three (for example, 'I know the boy what was here,' 'I know the boy who was here,' or 'I know the boy which was here'), having the child apply rules to unique material[4] (for example, Noun plus unique Verb in various contexts), having children answer questions about utterances (for example, 'The boy who graduated from the school is on the corner,' 'Where is the school?'), and having children reproduce utterances containing varying grammatical structures and nongrammatical structures. These approaches can be used to evaluate competence in the syntactic, semantic, and phonological components of the grammar.

The two studies that will be discussed now were attempts to discover how utterances composed of varying grammatical structures are understood and reproduced by children at different ages. A comparison was made of the kinds of structures understood and reproduced and those spontaneously produced by the children. The technique that was used was to ask subjects to immediately recall utterances presented to them by the experimenter.

It is probable that when you ask subjects to immediately recall utterances they will attempt to imitate what is presented to them, and that the results you obtain are merely imitations rather than reproductions of what is comprehended. The result might be similar to that obtained when you ask subjects to reproduce an utterance from an unknown language. If reproduction is strictly uncomprehending imitation and the subjects are speakers of any human language, they should be able to reproduce sounds, words, phrases, and sentences. The primary limitation on what they reproduce should be that of memory span and therefore, sentence length should be highly critical in success of repetition. If the utterance exceeds the subject's memory span there should be first certain omissions which occur and then substitutions. However, if modifications occur one might also assume that these modifications are due to how the utterance is understood and regenerated by the listener. Therefore, some evidence would be obtained about the kinds of structures that are understood and about the kinds of structures that are used to generate paraphrases or paraphrase-like utterances of the utterances that are presented for repetition.

4.2 Grammatical Competence in Normal-Speaking Children

The first study consisted of an evaluation of the kinds of responses obtained from preschool children and kindergarten children to a list of sentences which were exemplars of the syntactic structures and approximate structures discussed in the previous chapter. Because of the results of this study, the experiment was repeated with preschool and kindergarten children, limiting the sentence types presented for repetition. The list of completely well-formed sentences contained three exemplars each of a preselected subset of structures (those most frequently modified in the first study), and the list of not completely well-formed sentences contained exemplars of a preselected subset of approximate structures (the most and least frequently corrected in the first study). In addition to the repetition of these two lists, the children in the second study were asked to "correct" the sentences containing the approximate structures and to repeat the sentences containing exemplars of the well-formed syntactic structures presented to them in reverse word order. All sentences were selected from the language sample obtained from children.

The experimental procedure, a detailed description of the population, and the statistical results of these studies appear elsewhere.[5] Therefore, only a summary of the results will appear here. The modifications of utterances produced by children, merely summarized in the other publications, will be discussed in detail here.

Responses to lists of utterances were categorized as follows: a repetition when the subject repeated the transformation type or the nongrammatical structure in the sentence, a modification when any change in the syntactic structure occurred in the well-formed sentences, and a correction when the nongrammatical form was changed to a grammatical form. An example of modification is simplification of Nominalization to present tense: "She does the shopping and cooking and baking" to "She shops and cooks and bakes."[6] An example of a correction would be to reproduce "He wash his dirty face" as "He washes (or washed) his dirty face." Both spontaneous corrections (subjects produced corrections although they were only asked to repeat) as well as nonspontaneous corrections (subjects were asked to correct nongrammatical sentences) occurred. The statistical results are summarized in Figure 4.1. The mean percentage of items responded to by modification of structures, spontaneous corrections, and nonspontaneous corrections, for each six-month period over the age range, is shown. Significantly more of the structures were modified, and significantly more of the nongrammatical structures were spontaneously corrected by the 34-39-month-old children than by the 52-57-month-old children (youngest preschoolers versus oldest preschoolers). Significantly more of the structures were modified by 52-57-month-old children than by the 70-75-month-old children (oldest preschoolers versus oldest kindergartners) while significantly more of the nongrammatical structures were corrected when asked for (nonspontaneous corrections) by the 70-75-month-old children than by the 52-57-month-old children.

With reverse word order sentences there were no significant differences between the groups although more of the items were repeated by the older children than by the younger children. However, only a mean 20 per cent of the items were repeated by the oldest group of children.[7]

The most significant finding was that the structure of a particular sentence determined whether or not it was repeated, not its length. The correlation between sentence length and nonrepetition of sentences in their correct grammatical order is .03. For reverse word order utterances, on the other hand, the correlation is .87. The results of these studies indicated that repetition was dependent on structure rather than just

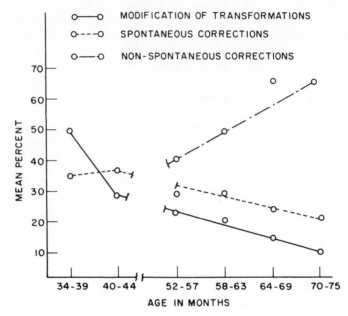

Figure 4.1 Mean percentage of children modifying transformational structures, spontaneously correcting nongrammatical structures, and correcting nongrammatical structures in sentences when asked to do so at various age levels.

imitation up to the limits of memory capacity. With sentences up to nine words in length, the length of the sentence was not the factor which determined successful repetition even for children as young as 3 years. The differences in the ability of children of varying ages to repeat sentence types was dependent on the particular rules used to generate these sentences, not length. When the structure was broken down completely, however (sentences in reverse word order), sentence length was a highly significant factor. Under this condition subjects imitate without comprehension, for the most part, and therefore repeat up to the limits of their memory capacity.[8]

In addition to the statistical trends observed, the hypothesis that repetition is dependent on the rules in the listener's grammar rather than being mere imitation, only limited by memory span, is further strengthened by the kinds of responses obtained in the repetition of certain structures. In the original study and in the following replication study the most frequent deviations found from complete repetition of a sentence were modifications of transformational structures and spontaneous corrections of nongrammatical forms. They were not omission of parts of sentences (that is, forgetting bits of the utterances), or even substitution of Prepositions, Articles, etc. In fact, there were no significant differences found between the groups in each of the studies in the mean number of items in which omission, complete or partial, or substitution took place.

The correlation between repetition and use was derived by comparing the structures repeated with those found in the language sample of either the same children, as in the first study, or children in the same age range, as in the second study. The syntactic structures which were used and repeated were significantly correlated for all groups. The modifications of transformational structures observed were either simplifications or those deviations from the completely well-formed structures found in the language sample.

The most frequently modified structures were those which involve expansions of the Verb Phrase, Conjunctions other than 'and,' and embedding. Table 4.1 lists the structures which were modified by 25 per cent or more of the children during the young nursery school period (age 2 years, 10 months to 3 years, 8 months, hereafter referred to as YNS), during the old nursery school period (age 4 years, 4 months to 5 years, 3 months hereafter referred to as ONS), and during the kindergarten period (age 5 years, 4 months to 6 years 3 months). They are listed in rank order of frequency of modification.

The operations of expansion of Verb Phrase, conjunction of sentences using Conjunctions other than 'and,' and embedding sentences all show significant changes in numbers of children using these structures from early preschool through first grade (age 2 years, 10 months to 7 years, 1 month). Despite the significant correlation between use and repetition more children in all groups are able to repeat sentences containing the above structures than to use them in the sentences they spontaneously generate. Older children are proportionately better at this task than are

Table 4.1
Structures Modified by 25 Per Cent or More of the Children

YNS N=14	ONS N=43	Kindergarten N=43
Auxiliary have	Have Got	Have Got
Conjunction So	Auxiliary Have	Auxiliary Have
Conjunction Cause	Nominalization	
Have Got	Conjunction Cause	
Nominalization		
Question		

younger children. However, even the oldest children in this study continue to modify structures, and, again, the modifications one observes are those which are found in the sentences produced by these children.

The three exemplars of the Auxiliary Have construction were the following:

1. I've been thinking about that.
2. I've already been there.
3. I've been sick for two weeks.

The most frequent modifications for all groups of children of this structure are the following in rank order of frequency. The period in which the type of modification most frequently occurs is indicated.

1. Omission of contracted form of have (YNS) "I been . . ."
2. Expansion of contracted form of have (Kinder) "I have been . . ."
3. Substitution of another form of past tense (ONS, not at all in YNS) "I was . . ."
4. Substitution of Aux 'be' for 'have' (ONS) "I'm been or I am been . . ."
5. Redundant use of 'have' "I've already've been . . ." (Kinder only)
6. Redundant use of 'be' "I've been already been . . ." (Kinder only)

The three exemplars of the Have Got construction were the following:

1. He's got magic beans.
2. I've got a lollipop.
3. We've got Chinese food.

The most frequent modifications for all groups of children of this structure are the following in rank order of frequency.

1. Omission of contracted form of 'have' or 'has' (in all age groups) "He got . . . , I got . . . , We got . . ."
2. Omission of 'got' (ONS) "He has . . . , I have, We have . . ."
3. Third person singular, present tense marker attached to 'got' (ONS) "He gots . . ."
4. Expansion of contracted form of 'have' (ONS) "He has got, I have got, We have got . . ."

The exemplars of conjunction included three instances of 'so,' 'if,' and 'because' Conjunctions. The following exemplars are one instance of each:

1. He hurt me so I hurt him back.
2. He's got to stay if he's not good.
3. He'll eat the ice cream because he wants to.

The most frequent modifications for all groups of children of these structures are the following in rank order of frequency.

1. Conjunction substituted by 'and' (YNS) "He hurt me and . . ."
2. Omission of S1 or S2 (YNS, not at all in Kinder) "I hurt him back." "He's got to stay."
3. Two sentences (that is, omission of any Conjunction) (ONS)
4. Nonobservation of Pronoun restrictions[9] (ONS) "I'll give it to you if I want it." "He hurt me so he hurt him back."
5. Nonobservation of Verb tense restriction (ONS) "I'll give it to you if you wanted it."

In addition to the above modifications a frequent occurrence in the YNS period was modification of "He'll eat . . ." to "He'll eats . . ." indicating that the contracted modal form may in some instances be an alternate form of the Pronoun, a grammatical occurrence found in early sentences. In opposition to this, a frequent occurrence during the ONS period was expansion of "He'll eat . . ." to "He will eat . . ." indicating that at this developmental stage the modal is indeed a structure always used in the base structure rules. Note that the expansion of the contracted form of 'have' in the Auxiliary Have construction occurs most frequently in the kindergarten period indicating that children at this stage do indeed have this class in their base structure rules.

There were three exemplars each of Participial Complement and Nominalization given for repetition. The following are examples of the two types of structures:

1. I like playing the piano.
2. Doing that is not nice.

The most frequent modification of the Participial Complement structure by the children in the YNS group was Infinitival Complement ("I like to play the piano"), and the most frequent modification of the Nominalization structure was present tense or Present Participle construction of the nominalized Verb or Verbs "He does that" or ("He's doing that.") Modification of the Participial Complement to an Infinitival Complement occurred infrequently in the other two groups but somewhat more frequently in the ONS group than in the kindergarten group. In the ONS group the most frequent modification of the Nominalization structure was reproduction of the embedded sentence with the Verb (or Verbs) in present tense. In the kindergarten group the most frequent modification was a Present Participle construction in the embedded sentence. Another modification, although infrequent, was omission of a sentence in the Complement construction ("I like it" for "I like playing the piano," or "I see someone" for "I see someone reading a book.")

These observations can be made from this analysis of the kinds of repetition of structures the children produced. The first is that the modifications were generated by rules which are in all instances simpler than those used in the sentences presented, and in some instances they represent approximations to the complete set of rules needed to generate the sentences presented. They are, however, for the most part, meaning preserving of at least one part of the message. Second, the modifications produced were very similar to the kinds of structures these children were using in their spontaneously generated sentences. One could observe developmental changes in the reproduction of structures over the age range that coincided with developmental changes observed in their spontaneous language. The indication is that in many instances these children were using the same rules to reproduce sentences as they used to generate sentences. However, in some instances they were better able to reproduce certain structures than use them in their spontaneous language. This result indicates that these structures are understood as having a certain underlying description. Although the child cannot as yet use the rules, in the generation of sentences, he understands them. Repetition, therefore, in conjunction with an analysis of spontaneous generation seems to be a technique that can be used for eliciting information about level of grammatical development. It gives us information about the kinds of structures the child has acquired and those that he is in the process of acquiring and the level of acquisition of those structures that he is in the process of acquiring. More importantly, the results of these studies indicate that the child does not listen passively to the language in his linguistic environment, attempting merely to reproduce only what he can remember of what he has heard, but, rather, actively goes through a process of matching what he hears to structures that he has internalized in order to regenerate or generate sentences.

The corrections observed in the reproduction of nongrammatical sentences reinforces this conclusion. There were interesting differences in the kinds of corrections which occurred over the age range. The sentence exemplars of nongrammatical structures are listed below with the most frequent type of modification for each group of children. In most instances these modifications are corrections, but in some few instances they are not. These occurrences are indicated by an asterisk. Where a correction took place both spontaneously and nonspontaneously, the correction was usually the same. Therefore the modifications listed refer to both types of corrections. A 0 indicates that no corrections occurred.

	YNS	ONS	Kinder
1. He wash his dirty face.	washes	washed	washed
2. They sleeping in their beds.	are	they're	they're
3. They get mad and then they pushed him.	push	got	got
4. The barber cut off his hair off.	-final 'off'	-final 'off'	all his hair off
5. I want to go New York in the morning.	+to	+to	+to
6. He likes to look at	+it	+Pronouns other than it (him, her, them)	
7. My daddy has new office down town.	+a	+a	+a
8. He growed bigger and bigger.	grow*	did grow	grew
9. He liketed that funny game.	liked	liked	liked
10. The little boy is washing hisself.	0	himself his body, face etc.	himself
11. You pick up it.	it up	it up	it up
12. What name you're writing?	are you	are you	are you
13. There's three trees.	are	are	are
14. Two brothers and one sister I have.	Brothers and sisters that I have	Inversion	Inversion
15. Don't put the hat.	+on	+on/away on the floor, on you	+on
16. I want a milk.	-a	-a/some, the, a glass of	some, the, a glass of
17. He took me at the circus today.	to	to	to
18. Where are the peoples?	-s	-s	-s
19. Mommy was happy so he kissed Betty.[10]	she	she	she
20. The teacher writes that numbers.	those	those	those

21.	It isn't any more rain.	no more rain*	there	there
22.	You can't put no more water in it.	any	-no/any	any
23.	He took the knife from falling.	0	from N (ex: John)*	and he is falling*
24.	This dress green.	0	is	is
25.	She took it away the hat.	-it	-it	-it

The choice of correction reflects, in many instances, the level of grammatical competence of the groups. For example, in corrections of sentence 1, the YNS children correct Verb form omission with a present tense marker whereas the children in the two older groups correct this nongrammatical form with a past tense marker. Sentence 16 is corrected by omission of the article by YNS children whereas ONS children correct with equal frequency by omission of the Article and selection of a determiner which meets selectional restrictions, and kindergarten children correct only by selection of an appropriate determiner. Sentence 23 is simply repeated by YNS children (it is, perhaps, from their point of view, within the realm of possibility) whereas the children in the two older groups have determined that it is nongrammatical and attempt to correct the nongrammaticality with the rules in their grammar. The structure "from falling" is a Nominalization structure and therefore used very infrequently by these groups of children. The ONS children observe certain selectional restrictions of the sentence (took X from) and substitute a possible Noun. The kindergarten children, however, have in addition observed the verbal property of 'falling' and attempt to maintain this property in their correction, reflecting a deeper analysis of the sentence that has been presented. Most of the differences in corrections observed between groups seem to be representative of this deeper and more elaborated analysis. Table 4.2 presents the nongrammatical structures *spontaneously corrected* by 25 per cent or more of the children in each group. They are listed in rank order of frequency of occurrence of correction. The sentence containing the approximate form is indicated on the left.

Most of the spontaneous corrections by 25 per cent or more of the children in the total population are of base structure rules. Transformational corrections follow in terms of total number and then correction of nongrammatical morphological structures. The balance however, changes somewhat over the age range. The young nursery school children most frequently correct base structure deviant rules. The kindergarten children's spontaneous corrections are equally divided between base structure rules and transformational deviant rules.

Table 4.2

Structures Spontaneously Corrected by 25 Per Cent or More of the Children

YNS	ONS	Kindergarten
5. Preposition O	5. Preposition O	5. Preposition O
6. NP O	7. Article O	3. Tense in Conj.
1. Vform O	1. Vform O	7. Article O
2. Aux O	2. Aux O	12. No Question
4. Particle R	12. No Question	4. Particle R
3. Tense in Conj.	21. There insertion	1. Vform O
22. 2X Neg.	4. Particle R	25. N P R
19. Pronoun in Conj.	3. Tense in Conj.	9. Vform R
20. Determiner N	16. Article S	19. Pronoun Conj.
25. NP R	25. NP R	10. Reflexive
18. Nform R		

The younger the children are the more frequent the spontaneous correc-tions. It has been postulated (1) that the older the child is, the more task-oriented he is and, therefore, the more frequently does he do what he is asked to despite the distraction of the stimulus (that is, a nongrammat-ical sentence) and (2) that the younger the child is, the more externalized are the rules of his grammar and, therefore, the more frequently does he 'hear' and reproduce sentences in terms of these rules disregarding their exact form. The latter holds true despite the fact that he more often spontaneously produces these deviancies. We also have evidence of this in the modification of certain structures when reproducing the fully grammatical sentences. The YNS children more frequently modify struc-tures by using more elementary rules. This give us some evidence that this is what the child does when he listens to sentences in his environment.

In the case of nonspontaneous corrections, that is, asked-for corrections, a very different picture emerges. The older children much more frequently corrected nongrammatical forms. Almost all of the exemplars of nongram-matical structures were corrected by at least 25 per cent of the kinder-garten children. Table 4.3 presents those structures not corrected by at least 25 per cent of the ONS and kindergarten children. The sentence containing the approximate form is indicated on the left.

Not only were there more frequent corrections by the older children when they were asked to do so but the younger children, in a significantly greater number of instances ($p < .001$) than older children, did not correct structures they had previously spontaneously corrected. The task was put to them as "I'm saying something wrong. How should I say that?" Their concept of "wrong" was not always concerned with the question of gram-

Table 4.3

Structures Not Corrected in Nonspontaneous Corrections by at Least 25 Per Cent of Children

ONS	Kindergarten
23. VP S	23. VP S
14. S-O Inversion	13. Vnumber Inversion
13. Vnumber Inversion	14. S-O Inversion
19. Pronoun in Conj.	
3. Tense in Conj.	
17. Preposition S	
8. Vform S	

maticality, although this was always the case with older children. The younger children, in their efforts to correct the sentences, sometimes carefully articulated each word in the utterance, sometimes said it as loudly as they could or generated a new utterance. Examples of the latter response are the following:

"They washed up" for 'They sleeping in their beds.'
"He loved it" for 'He liketed that funny game.'
"This dress will be light green" for 'This dress green.'

These younger children obviously had the complete set of rules in their grammar for such structures as tense restriction in conjunction, as evidenced by their spontaneous corrections, but when specifically asked to apply them did not seem to understand what was required or could not do so.

In addition to the corrections of nongrammatical utterances, modifications such as those encountered in the repetition of the completely well-formed sentences, and similar to structures found in the generation of spontaneous sentences, were found. For example, Verb form omissions, substitutions, and redundancies occurred ("grow," "growded," and "grewed" for the nongrammatical 'growed' in sentence 8 occurred. Again, these modifications reflect various levels of grammatical competence. "Grow" was used most frequently in the YNS group, and "grewed" outside of correction, was used most frequently in the kindergarten group.

More carefully controlled studies, which concentrate on specific aspects of grammatical competence such as types of rules, properties of lexical items in the strings, selectional restrictions, etc., will give us better cues about the parameters of grammatical competence during the acquisition and elaboration periods. It is necessary to document the fact that some structures appear earlier or are understood earlier. However, examination in depth of these structures must be undertaken so that logical explanations for this early or late occurrence are available.

Thus far the repetition of the reverse word order sentences has been mentioned only in terms of the fact that sentence length was significantly correlated with correct repetition unlike the case of grammatical sentences, where sentence length played a nonsignificant role in sentence repetition. Also, the fact that there were no significant differences between groups in success of repetition with reverse word order sentences was mentioned. Other kinds of behavior noted in the repetition of these items indicate an attempt to find some grammatical structure in the sentences. In the presentation of these items for repetition the string was phrased, grouping words in the string together, as one would, if they had been in correct order in the sentence. The following are some examples:

1. Lollipop a / got I've.
2. Water more some / have I can?
3. That about thinking / been I've.

These strings, therefore, were not read as a list of non-associated words, but read with intonation and stress as near normal as possible. It is probably for this reason that some repetitions of these strings contained grammatical inversions and some repetitions were echos of the intonational and stress pattern of the sentence with the neutral vowel 'shwa' (uh) substituted for the morphemes. The above three exemplar sentences were repeated in the following manner to produce grammatical inversions.

1. Lollipop I've got I've.
2. Water can I have.
3. That uh I've been thinking.

A longer string such as 'Him hit he/ so him saw he' was reproduced in some instances as *"uh* uh uh/ uh *uh* uh uh" (with the falling intonation found in declarative sentences). It is possible that breaking the string into phrases allowed the children to code bits and convert them into grammatical phrases. Never was a whole sentence converted. Giving the string a stress and intonational pattern seemed to give the children some information for coding and reproduction.

Table 4.4 gives the percentage of instances in which children in the ONS group and the kindergarten group responded to the inverted word order strings with an echo of the stress and intonation pattern or a grammatical inversion or complete omission (refusal to respond at all). As can be seen, the younger children more frequently than the older children responded with an echo response than a grammatical inversion, while the reverse was true of the older children. Also, the younger children, in twice as many

Table 4.4

Types and Percentages of Responses to Reverse Word Order Sentences

	ONS	Kindergarten
Echo	14%	10%
Grammatical Inversion	10%	14%
Omission	10%	5%

instances as the older, did not respond at all. The differences found between grammatical inversion and echo responses between the two groups of children may be another indication of the greater grammatical competence of the older children who can or are paying more attention to the segmental features of the string rather than the suprasegmental features. As was noted in the discussion of early sentences, it is perhaps through the cues of intonation and stress that the child first acquires the concept "sentence." This aspect of repetition of stress and intonational pattern seems to be worthy of much more careful exploration over a long developmental period: from babbling to the use of polysyllabic words in sentences.

One other aspect of repetition of reverse word order sentences was observed. The largest proportion of errors was concerned with the final word in the string. In the ONS group 29 per cent of the errors were concerned with the first word, 33 per cent with the middle word/s, and 38 per cent with the last word. In the kindergarten group 22 per cent of the errors were concerned with the first word, 36 per cent with the middle word, and 42 per cent with the last word. This result seems to emphasize the fact that recall of these unstructured strings was being performed in a manner very different from that used in recall of sentences. The effort seemed to be primarily one of memorization and retention of the first things heard in the sequence rather than an analysis of the whole sequence or chunks of the whole sequence. The technique used in sentence recall seems to be the latter and whether it is whole or part seems to be dependent on the underlying structure of the sentence (multiple or single underlying strings).

The responses obtained from repetition of sentences and the comparison of these responses to those obtained in the repetition of reverse word order sentences clearly indicate that children do not listen passively to the sentences in their environment and attempt to merely memorize up to the limits of their memory capacity and then reproduce their memorizations. Even when actually asked to imitate, as in the repetition experiments, the children tended to reproduce sentences according to the rules in their grammar. Their sentence modifications were indeed reflections of their level of grammatical competence since the structures they modified and the kind of modifications used were analogous to the observations and analyses about grammatical development made from spontaneous productions. However, it was clear that their comprehension of structures and their acquisition of grammatical rules in some specifiable instances exceeded that observed in spontaneous productions. The spontaneous corrections of the younger children and the nonspontaneous corrections of the older children give us evidence for this assumption, and we have further evidence from the repetition of structures in the completely well-formed sentences where the children exceeded the competence displayed in their production in certain instances but only in certain instances. The structures reproduced in these instances were those which greater numbers of children in that age category were beginning to acquire, and were logical extensions of rules which were being used in their spontaneous generations (such as Conjunctions other than 'and'). We are beginning, then, to obtain answers about the role of imitation in language acquisition and the sequence and differences between comprehension and production. There are, however, too many aspects of the grammar intermingled in the stimulus sentences presented for repetition. A sharper focusing of the stimulus materials will perhaps give us clearer and more detailed answers.

4.3   Examining Grammatical Capacity

The most general view about grammatical capacity seems to be that the child has the mechanisms and procedures for acquisition of symbol systems and hypotheses formation which can then be applied in deriving the rules of a grammar. It has been stated that what these mechanisms are or how they operate in the nervous system is not understood. We can describe the product of this capacity at various stages of development, and its outcome—the acquisition of the basic grammatical rules of the language, a further elaboration of these rules, and a continuing and deepening analysis of how these rules are used in specific instances with all types of lexical items. The study of the exceptional or deviant child and the comparison of the "normal" and deviant child in the process of language acquisition and development may help us to determine what these mechanisms and procedures are, or the bases of grammatical capacity.

In some instances, with exceptional children, there may be a primary determining factor which is understood and logically leads to a language deviancy, as in the case of the deaf child. There are obviously many factors outside of deafness which, even in the case of the deaf "only" child (meaning no other problems such as mental retardation, brain damage, etc.), which may contribute to differences within this group in linguistic capacity, competence, and production. To give one example, the age of onset of deafness, it has been noted, plays a critical role in the course of language development. This is a factor, however, which is measurable and can be weighed in the evaluation of grammatical capacity. We can then determine the weight of ± hearing (degree and nature of hearing loss)[12], age of onset (before or after age 2, before or after age 4, etc.), ± other factors, (intelligence, parental attitude, etc.), to evaluate the contribution of hearing loss to the types of grammars that are acquired by these children. It is *not* being implied that this is a simple-minded procedure. One of the most complicating factors is that the product of *all* factors may introduce another factor which is not being measured by this parcelling procedure. However, the possibility of such an evaluation exists and would lead to a greater understanding of the mechanisms and procedures used in language acquisition *and* to a greater understanding of the educational problems of these children. The procedure might be somewhat as follows:

Child X± a, b, c, etc. ⟶ Linguistic Comprehension and Production Y
Y± a, b, c, etc. ⟶ Linguistic Capacity Z± a, b, c, etc.

Measures of linguistic competence, Y, can be obtained by a systematic description of the grammatical rules in all three components of the grammar (syntax, semantics, and phonology) that the child can spontaneously produce and comprehend.[13] A comparison of these children's performance and the normal-speaking child's performance at various stages of development would indicate differences in linguistic capacity; that is, the capacity to determine the functional relationships, the classes in the language, properties of members of a class, and rules of cooccurrence which may be considered to be the universal aspects of language.

In some other instances children exhibit some degree of language deviancy which may range from not speaking at all to one sound substitution, and we cannot determine the primary factor or factors which contribute to this deviancy. There are no obvious physiological or environmental determinants. In these instances an evaluation of linguistic competence may lead to a determination of these factors. The procedure might be as follows: Linguistic Comprehension and Production Y ± a, b, c, etc. ⟶ Linguistic Capacity Z ± a, b, c, etc. ⟶ Child X ± a, b, c, etc.

The experimental conditions under which these measures are obtained (the nature of the task given to the child) may point to particular deficits in the child's capacity to perceive, identify, recall, and form hypotheses about significant linguistic generalizations.

In the first type of instance we are evaluating the relationship of a described mechanism to a certain linguistic capacity which we hope to determine. In the second type of instance we are attempting to determine the factors which may be contributing to a certain linguistic capacity which we can describe.

The possibility of obtaining measures of linguistic competence and capacity and 'general' capacities depends, of course, on our ability to devise appropriate measurement techniques. We are a long way from accomplishing this task.

The experiment to be described concerns a population of children whose language deviancy could not be traced to a physiological or environmental factor or factors in any definitive manner. Some of the statistical data obtained from a comparison of the grammar of this group of children and the grammar of a normal-speaking population are reported elsewhere.[14] In this discussion these children's grammatical capacity, as shown in their comprehension and production of syntactic structures, will be examined. How their linguistic capacity might be related to the mechanisms and procedures for the acquisition of language, which we would like to isolate and describe, will be explored.

The language usage of this group of children had been labeled as 'infantile,' implying that they were producing language which, to the labeler, was deemed more appropriate for a younger group of children. This, in turn, might imply that it was taking longer for these children to proceed through the *usual* sequences of language acquisition than it does for normal-speaking children, but that they were nevertheless going through the normal sequence.

The children in this population ranged in age from 3,0 years to 5,11 years. They were matched to a normal-speaking population by age, sex, and I.Q. To examine language production, language was obtained under the same stimulus conditions previously described in the first chapter. In addition to an analysis of the language samples produced by these children, they were also asked to repeat lists of grammatical and nongrammatical sentences in the manner described in the earlier section of this chapter. Therefore, an examination of both their linguistic production and an aspect of comprehension was carried out.

In the analysis of the language produced by these children and by the normal-speaking population two factors emerged. The first factor is that at any age level throughout the range the syntactic structures as a whole being used by these children did not match structures being used by normal-speaking younger children. Therefore, the label 'infantile' was being used inappropriately. The second factor is that all the children in the so-labeled group were producing similar types of structures regardless of their age (that is, 3 years, 4 years, or even 5 years, 11 months). Therefore, the implication that these children were simply slower in going through the usual sequences of language acquisition is incorrect, within the limits of the age range examined. Unfortunately, these children were not followed longitudinally, so that further development beyond the last age at which they were observed was not explored. This of course would be a most valuable study.

Despite the fact that the label applied to the group was found to be inappropriate, these children were producing language which was considered deviant by the adult native speakers of their language, and they were being grouped by this deviancy. An attempt was made to determine what the parameters of this language deviancy were and whether or not these parameters were, indeed, characteristic of each member of this group by structural descriptions of their utterances. The fact that it was more difficult to understand what these children were saying than it was with their normal-speaking age peers might be accounted for by the sound changes they made in their production of morphemes. There were, in fact, some generalizations that could be found in these sound changes which were characteristic of all the members of the group. However, their language deviancy could not be described simply in terms of the phonological rules they used. In addition to these, there were certain differences in the syntactic rules underlying the sentences they produced which were also characteristic of all members of the group and led to their categorization as a group.

At first glance many of the sentences produced by these children seem to be echoes of the early sentences produced by normal-speaking children, which probably accounts for the fact that their language had been labeled as 'infantile.' There are two aspects of their language production and the rules postulated to describe this production which makes the term 'infantile' misleading. First, the 3,0-year-old using deviant language is using structures which are more sophisticated than those used by a normal-speaking 2,0-year-old in a comparative analysis. The 2-year-old is producing sentences whose underlying structure could be described as Marker + Topic + Modifier. The 3-year-old who is described as using 'infantile' language is producing sentences which can be described as NP + VP and expansions of NP + VP. For example in NP expansion we see Determiner + N ("My mommy . . .") and in VP expansion we see V + NP or V + Object (". . . make eggs.")

The following are some sentences taken from a conversation by the 2-year-old and the 3-year-old who is using deviant language, which are exemplars of this difference in the underlying structure of their sentences:

2-year-old	*3-year-old*
Daddy wash hands.	You have his one.
Nose hurt you?	Me have this one.
Bunting hurt you?	This babie's.
Chair's broken.	That hard.
Get down.	Want take this?
Cat right back.	I good.
See snow?	This good?
See the no (snow).	I take this one.
At's right.	I working.
At's a book.	My mommy make eggs.
Show you book mommy?	I make daddy pie.

On the other hand, the normal-speaking child, whose sentences we have listed above, at age 3.0, is far more sophisticated than the deviant-speaking child in grammatical production and, we would suggest, competence as well. The following are some examples of declarative, negative, and question sentences taken from the conversation of the two children:

Normal-speaking 3,0	*Deviant-speaking 3,0*
Do you see it over there?	Which mine?
I want the fire engine to talk.	I go wash hands.
He's going up the ladder.	He's go there.
There's a fire and here's the ladder.	My like gun.
The monster's not coming.	Not take mine.
He isn't coming.	This is not buttoned.

In addition if we look at the WH Question, Negation, and Infinitival Complement constructions of the deviant-speaking population we see that there is not much difference between the 3-year-old's productions and the almost 6-year-old's productions. These types of sentences were being produced consistently rather than in alternation with completely well-formed utterances.

Age	Question	Negation	Infinitival Complement
3,0	Where hang it?	Not take mine.	I know ride no feet.
3,6	How that wheel come round?	Him not feel good.	Him want go.
4,0	Why you put?	He not like Tippy.	Him going walk.
4,6	How you polish yourself?	Not any more pictures.	He want shoot.
5,1	What you do with this?	No itch himself.	He want look Blacky doing.

5,6   Why him take out whip?   Him not try.   He like bite.
5,11 How it turn off?   Blacky not talk.   Him try push a dog.

There were, in addition, systematic speech sound substitutions in these children's productions of morphemes. For example, the last sentence in the Negation column was produced as "Blaty not talt."

Rather than stating that these children's language production was infantile or slower in going through the normal course of development, one is led to state that their language production is arrested at "some stage" of development. The years from 2 to 4 are those in which dramatic changes occur in the language production of normal-speaking children. It is during the early part of these years that one begins to observe sentences which incorporate the expansion of base structure rules and use of the elementary transformations in their completed form. In the latter part of these years one sees the increasing use of transformations which involve the embedding of sentences into other sentences and certain types of conjunctions. From age 6 to 7 one could observe another dramatic change in the *elaboration* of the basic syntactic structures. Since this is a horizontal rather than a longitudinal study, it is impossible to state that the children who were then almost 6 were producing the same structures at age 3 or 4. However, it can be stated that at any age throughout the age range of this population the same types of sentences were being produced. We also cannot answer a most interesting and perhaps vital question in terms of understanding the mechanisms and procedures of language acquisition. We cannot describe the grammar of these same children at age 8 or 12, etc. We will, however, attempt an explanation of the differences in grammatical capacity that these sentences seem to reflect and a description of the stage of grammatical competence at which the arrest referred to seems to have taken place.

As was stated earlier, the sentences which were being produced could not be described as the use of the earliest type of rules (S $\rightarrow$ (Modifier) Topic + Intonational Marker), but they can be described with rules which describe somewhat later sentences where the Subject-Object relationship is established. That is, S $\rightarrow$ NP + VP, S $\rightarrow$ NP + V + NP. If one were to describe a basically useful grammar in English, one which conveys "sufficient meaning," it would be a grammar consisting of the above rules (including, of course, the expansions of NP and VP cited, that is, Determiner and Negative and Question morphemes). The sentences which have been categorized under the headings of Question, Negation, and Infinitival Complement are all interpretable and, for the most part, nonambiguous. To oversimplify, the sentences produced seem to be reflections of a basic "unmarked" grammar perhaps universal in nature.

The WH Question sentences seem to be of the form Q + NP + VP with simply a WH attachment rule. The Negation sentences seem to be of the form NP + Neg. + VP with simply a Neg. hopping rule. The Infinitival Complement constructions seem to be of the form NP + VP + VP. Outside of these basic structures, which are nevertheless of primary importance in conveying meaning, the productive rules in these children's grammar is quite limited.

In terms of NP expansion into Determiner + Noun, the possessive class (my and your), the demonstratives (this and that), and the quantifiers (some and no) all occur, but frequently without observation of restrictions on cooccurrence. On the other hand Articles are much more frequently omitted than used, so that it seems that this class of determiner is not in the grammar, or, to put it in other terms, that it is a basically understood category and therefore need not be produced in sentences as the other determiners must (that is, it is a redundant class). Copula constructions occur but occur so randomly that it would seem that they are a part of the NP rather than a separate class for these children. One frequently observes sentences such as the following: "This good," "Him wolfie," and much less frequently, "That's mine" and "What's this," indicating that the latter may be memorized items.

The Verb Phrase is almost never expanded into Modal + Verb. The one exception is the contracted form of 'will' as in "I'll write my name," but to postulate a separate category in the grammar of these children for the Modal 'will' seems unjustified since it never appears in question or negative sentences. It may possibly be that the tense aspect of this construction is marked in these children's grammar but this seems unlikely since tense is seldom marked in sentences.

Verb Phrase is also almost never expanded into 'be' + Present Participle + Verb. Various forms of this construction appear: "I going" or "He' put." This form as well as 'I'll' may be alternate memorized forms (that is 'he' or 'he's'). Very infrequently forms such as "I'm sitting" are produced. A construction such as 'he's put' never appears in the sentences produced by normal-speaking children aged 3 to 7 years in this population, even by the youngest of these children. "He's puts," however, does appear. Constructions such as "I going" also appear in the language sample of the normal-speaking population but in alternation with the completed structure "I'm sitting," whereas with the children in the deviant-speaking population the completed structure is the exception rather than the rule.

Verb Phrases were modified by Adverbials of the type 'too,' 'now,' 'here' and 'there.' These modifiers can be described as basically critical in conveying "sufficient" meaning. Occasionally Prepositional Phrases were used. Sentences with particles of the type "How it turn off" and "How that wheel come round" are produced. However, frequently the introductory Preposition in a Prepositional Phrase is omitted as in "He's dat house" and "I'm fall floor." Prepositions, then, may be a property attached to Verbs rather than a category in the grammar. The Verb 'go,' for example, may be stored in the grammar as 'go to,' the Verb 'fall' as 'fall on,' etc., and Verb + Particle constructions entered as a single item in the dictionary. Sentences involving the separation transformation ("Me took it off") were produced by some of these children but always involved V-it-particle. These may therefore be memorized structures. The marked Pronouns (him, me, her) and the unmarked Pronouns (he, I, she) are used in alternation. However, the marked Pronoun is used much more frequently than the unmarked. It may be that, for generative purposes, there is no separate class in the grammar of these children labeled 'Pronoun.' Since all subject Pronouns are marked as well as object Pronouns, all Pronouns may be categorized as Nouns in the grammar.

We have noted certain omissions in the sentences produced by these children in base structure and morphological rules. In the sentences produced by the normal-speaking population certain omissions were also observed. However, unlike the case with normal-speaking children, where omission and other deviant forms or approximations to completely well-formed structures occurred in alternation with completed forms, some of the deviant forms were used almost solely by these children. Figure 4.2 presents the mean per cent of frequency of usage of deviant forms in the utterances produced by the children in both groups and the percentage of children in both groups using the various deviant forms. Not only were the deviant forms used significantly more frequently by the deviant-speech group but the most frequently used form was omission of a rule. As we noted in the discussion of base structure rules and morphological rules, nonexpansion of a symbol in the base structure string is the most elementary type of approximation to the completed structure and occurs most frequently with the youngest children in the age range of the normal-speaking population. With the normal-speaking children this was a stage of development in the acquisition of a class. With the deviant-speaking children this seems to be *the* stage of development, that is, lack of a class.

As was indicated, most of the simple transformational structures produced by the children in the deviant speech group were generated by the operation of conjoining elements. There is some indication that the operations of permutation of elements is occurring in sentence generation but of a very restricted kind in the case of the youngest children in this group. The negative element hops and Adverb inversions occur in the sentences of some of these children but restrictions of Verb number (when the Verb

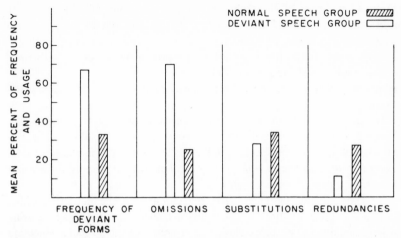

Figure 4.2 Mean percentage of frequency of deviant forms in the sentences produced by normal-speaking and deviant-speaking children and the mean percentage of children using morphological and base structure rules with omissions, substitutions, and redundancies in each group.

appears) is not observed. These may also be instances of memorized constructions.

Both 'conjunction' and 'embedding' are found in the sentences produced by some few of these children. However, conjunction is often of the form S^1 and S^2, without any evidence of any restrictions on agreement of Verb tense and number or sequential Pronoun. It seems to be simply a stringing together of two sentences by the morpheme 'and' or 'cause.' The Relative Clause construction produced by some of these children is always of the type NP + VP + NP and with a very restricted class of Verbs, limited in fact to 'know' and 'think' ("I know what you do"). These constructions also appear to be simply S1 + S2. Adjectives are used by all the children as are Nominal Compounds. Although the Adjectives that are used may be limited in number (no count was taken), they seem to cover a range (big, dirty, pink, etc.). The Possessive structure is not used by all the children and is often produced in some deviant manner ("That my", "Jody crayon here").

All of the children in the deviant speech group produce not completely well-formed negatives and questions, almost all of the time. Of the remaining structures derived from a single underlying string, a mean 48 per cent of these children produce these structures in a deviant form all of the time. The structures derived from multiple underlying strings are produced by a mean 42 per cent of these children in a deviant form all of the time. It must be kept in mind that far from all the children in the group are producing all simple or generalized transformational structures. Only a mean 47 per cent of these children are producing sentences with even approximate simple transformational structures and only a mean 43 per cent are producing sentences with approximate generalized transformations.

These children are observing and using some rules of structure in the language but these seem to be the most basic and generalized rules that can be derived. In some instances, as indicated, there is even some doubt that a generalization has been made. It may be that these are simply memorized forms.

In some of the sentences that the children in the deviant-speaking population produce there is also some evidence that they may be using rules or forming hypotheses about the structure of the language which are different from those of the normal-speaking population. Nevertheless, these utterances also seem to reflect the fact that certain types of generalizations are being made about their language by these children, although, in some instances, they are different from those made by normal-speaking children. These types of utterances did not occur frequently with this small sample of children, but certain types were used with consistency by particular children in the population. The following are some sample utterances:

1. No ride feet.
2. He'm put.
3. My like guns.
4. Any more not pictures?
5. Big the dog.

Given the context these can be translated as:

1. I ride without using feet.
2. He's putting.
3. I like guns.
4. Are there no more pictures?
5. The dog is big.

Both class and sequence rules are being violated by the above sentences. Some of the violations might be due to phonetic similarity as in 'my' and 'me' but for the most part this is not the case. Some possible very early sentences from a group of normal-speaking children wishing to convey the same meaning might be as follows:

6. (I) ride no feet.
7. He put.
8. (Me) like guns.
9. No more pictures?
10. Dog big.

The sentences 1 through 5, in some ways, are exemplars of greater grammatical sophistication than are the typical types of utterances of very young normal-speaking children. Certain classes of the language are appearing in these sentences which do not appear in the early sentences of normal-speaking children as for example 'any more,' the contracted form of the auxiliary Verb 'be' ('m) used independently as shown by its attachment to the Pronoun, and the Article 'the.' However, their use in these utterances seems to be evidence that certain basic restrictions on the use of these classes and the functional relationships expressed in their use have not been acquired, as they have by normal-speaking children, and appear to be the result of the earliest type of grammatical operation-conjunction.

1. ride feet + no
2. Any Pro. + any Aux
3. Me + I → My
4. Any more + not pictures
5. (It is) big + the dog

These structures not only represent different hypotheses about structures in the language, but these hypotheses may be a deterrent to further grammatical development. They may not only lead to incorrect conclusions but may also be blind alleys which do not form the basis for further expansion and deepening of grammatical analysis.

We cannot describe the types of generalizations these children are making in an even partially complete manner since the population is small and the data insufficient. It would be most appropriate to longitudinally follow the grammatical development of a group of these so-called "infantile speech" children to describe the hypotheses these children are making about language and where these hypotheses lead them. The important point is that not only is the language of these children different in some marked degree from our model of language, but it is also different in specific ways that we have incompletely described but which can be further described. These specific ways reflect the fact that, just as normal children form hypotheses about language, so do children who use deviant language. It is our task to discover what these hypotheses are.

There are some children whose language at age 5 or 6 presumably cannot be described as even approximating the grammar of the children described here. There are some children who do not speak at all. There are others, presumably, whose syntactic rules closely approximate those of normal-speaking children but whose use of phonological rules makes their language deviant. We need therefore, first, to describe the content and structure of deviant language patterns. We do not know enough about the content and structure of these patterns to correlate types of deviancy to degree of deviancy, although intuitive judgments of degree are continuously made. We would like, in fact, to discover what these correlations are. We may then determine some of the critical linguistic generalizations necessary for language comprehension in addition to determining the significant linguistic discriminations not being made by these children.

In our description of the types of utterances produced by the children in this population we postulated that certain structures were present and in the comparison of the utterances produced by these children and normal-speaking children we postulated that certain structures were absent and different. We further noted that, in the case of missing structures, not even some of these structures appeared in the utterances of the older children in this population but that the grammar remained quite static from age 3 to 6 years. However, our description dealt only with the types of utterances produced, not those comprehended. Also, as we stated earlier, the possible explanations for the language differences observed could not be described. These children, therefore, were asked to repeat lists of sentences with varying syntactic structures, as described in the earlier part of this chapter, to see if further information could be obtained about their grammatical competence and further insight gained about possible differences between them and normal-speaking children in the mechanisms used in language processing.

The statistical differences in the repetition of the two groups of children (normal- and deviant-speaking) could be accounted for primarily by omission. Significantly more of the deviant-speaking children repeated sentences with omission of phrases or with only the last words or, in some instances, omission of a whole sentence. Figure 4.3 presents the mean per cent of items repeated, repeated with omissions, and repeated with modifications other than omission by both groups of children. The category 'other modifications' includes substitutions, modifications of transformations, and corrections. Most of the modifications by the normal-speaking group could be accounted for by correction of nongrammatical utterances. Most of the modifications of the deviant-speaking group could be accounted for by nongrammatical modifications of transformations.

It will be recalled that the correlation between sentence length and nonrepetition of sentences was nonsignificant for the large population discussed in the previous section. This was also the case for the normal-

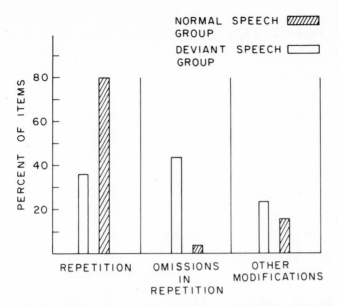

Figure 4.3 The percentage of sentences repeated, repeated with omissions and repeated with other modifications by normal-speaking children and deviant-speaking children.

speaking population matched with the deviant-speaking group and used for comparison (r = .04). On the other hand, the correlation between sentence length and nonrepetition of sentences was highly significant for the deviant population (r = .53, t = 4.5, p < .001). We may state, then, that the actual morpheme length of a sentence plays a vital role in success of repetition for this group of children. Further, when the omissions are examined more closely, we see that in most instances it is literally the beginning parts of the sentences which are omitted: the Subject, the Subject + Verb, sentence one of two conjoined sentences, and the sentence into which a second sentence is embedded. This is not always the case but it is most frequently the case. Therefore, the last things heard are most frequently recalled.

With the youngest child in the deviant-speech group (age 3,0) this type of behavior is most marked, and the exceptions are interesting. The following sentences are the list of completely grammatical sentences presented for repetition and the responses of the 3,0-year-old (A) and the oldest child in the group who was 5,11 years old (B).

1.   He was washed.
    (A) He wash.   (B) He was wash.

2. He isn't a good boy.
   (A) He not good boy.   (B) He not him good.

3. Are you nice?
   (A) Nice?   (B) You nice?

4. He'll be good.
   (A) He good.   (B) He be good.

5. Now I have kittens.
   (A) Kittens.   (B) Have kittens.

6. Where are you going?
   (A) You going?   (B) Where you go?

7. Don't use my dough.
   (A) and (B) No use my dough.

8. There isn't any more.
   (A) Isn't any more.   (B) Not it any more.

9. He took it off.
   (A) Took it off.   (B) Complete repetition

10. I've got a lollipop.
    (A) Lollipop.   (B) I got a lollipop.

11. He's not going to the party.
    (A) Not going.   (B) He not going.

12. I've already been there.
    (A) Been there.   (B) I been there.

13. I did read the book.
    (A) Read the book.   (B) I did read a book.

14. I'm writing daddy's name.
    (A) Writing daddy's name. (B) I writing daddy's name.

15. I cut myself.
    (A) and (B) Complete repetition.

16. Peter is over here and you are over there.
    (A) Over here.   (B) Peter over there. Peter over there.

17. I see a red book and a blue book.
    ` (A) I see blue book.   (B) I see a blue book.

18. I'll give it to you if you want it.
    (A) Want it.   (B) You want it.

19. He saw him so he hit him.
    (A) Hit.   (B) He hitted him.

20. He'll eat the ice cream because he wants to.
    (A) Wants to.   (B) I eat the ice cream cause I want.

21. David saw the bicycle and he was happy.
    (A) Happy.   (B) David see bicycle. He be happy.

22. I have a pink dog.
    (A) Pink dog.   (B) Complete repetition

23. I don't know what he's doing.
    (A) Doing.   (B) I don't know what him doing.

24. I want to play.
    (A) Want to play.   (B) Complete repetition

25. You have to drink milk to grow strong.
    (A) Drink milk.   (B) I had drink milk and grow strong.

26. She does the shopping and cooking and baking.
    (A) Baking.   (B) Doing shopping.

27. The baby carriage is here.
    (A) Here.   (B) The baby carriage here.

With most of the sentences the 3,0-year-old merely exactly replicates the last word or words. This occurs in nineteen of the twenty-seven sentences, indicating that in most instances the child is merely imitating rather than comprehending and reproducing the sentence. In only one instance is there complete repetition (sentence 15). This sentence contains only three morphemes. However, several other sentences containing only three morphemes are repeated by simple repetition of the last word (for example, sentence 3— Aux— Inversion Question) or by some modification (for example, sentence 1— Passive, sentence 4— Modal Will + Be). All Conjunction sentences, and Relative Clause and Nominalization sentences, that is, those involving operations on more than one underlying string, are replicated by repetition of the last word. Sentences involving permutation (for example, Aux Question, Adverb Inversion and WH Question sentences 3, 5, and 6) and expansion of the Verb Phrase (Have Got, Aux Have— and Aux Be— sentences 10, 12, and 14) are all repeated in the above manner. The Pronoun Subject is omitted in sentences 9 and 24, although the rest of the sentence is replicated. There are some sentences which are repeated with modifications indicating that some processing and perhaps matching to rules in the grammar may be going on (sentences 1, 2, 4, 7, 11, 17, and 25). Tense markers, auxiliaries, and modals are omitted but there are some aspects of these sentences which are being attended to and replicated. The negative element is always preserved when it appears. These sentences can be described as a stringing together of elements in the following manner:

S ⟶ NP VP (NP)
S ⟶ NEG (NP) VP
S ⟶ VP NP

Examples of the product of these structures are the following sentences:

1. He wash.
2. He not good boy.
4. He good.
7. No use my dough.
11. Not going.
17. I see blue book.
25. Drink milk.

These structures are very much like some of those being produced by this child spontaneously, but are only a limited number of the structures being spontaneously produced. The repetitions of the 5,11-year-old present a quite different pattern. This child is reproducing many of the sentences with modifications which indicate that in most instances some degree of comprehension and recoding for repetition is going on. This child does not merely imitate last things heard. In most instances the Auxiliary Verb, Modal, and Copula are omitted (for example, "wash" in sentence 1, "go" in sentence 6, Pronouns and Articles are omitted or substituted, and a Prepositional Phrase is omitted (sentence 11). However, Conjunctions are sometimes reproduced as two sentences. Pronoun and Verb tense restrictions are not observed in these instances, but attention is being paid to the fact that the sentence heard consists of two sentences. The Relative Clause construction is essentially replicated in sentence 23. Repetitions of sentences are quite consistent with the types of sentences being produced as described in the discussion of these children's spontaneous productions.

These children are limited in repetition not only by the length of the sentence but also by the depth or complexity of the sentence. Unlike the normal-speaking children, who could replicate certain structures which they did not spontaneously produce, these children either repeated with less structural complexity than exhibited in their spontaneous productions, as in the case of the 3,0-year-old, or repeated only nearly up to the level of the grammatical competence exhibited in their spontaneous productions, as in the case of the 5,11-year-old. And, of course, the level of complexity of the spontaneous productions of the 5,11-year-old was severely limited. In this child's repetitions the Aux-Inversion Question (sentence 3), the Adverb Inversion (sentence 5) and the Negation (sentence 7) as well as the Conjunction sentences were repeated with modifications reflecting the limitations of this child's grammar. However, repetition changed from mere imitation, for the most part, to the modifications in repetition observed over the age range of this small population.

In addition to these observations, further exemplars of types of structures which seem to be the exclusive formulations of this group of children appeared. The 3,0-year-old repeated so little that there were no such exemplars, although they were spontaneously produced by this child. The following are some exemplars from the 5,11-year-old child's repetitions:

2. He not him good.
8. Not it any more.
20. I eat ice cream cause I want.
25. I had milk and grow strong.

The results obtained from repetition of nongrammatical sentences are essentially the same as those described above. There were some corrections but only by the older children in the group. The Article 'the' is either omitted or consistently substituted by 'a.' Pronoun Subjects in conjunction are substituted usually by 'I' or 'me.' Auxiliaries, modals and copulas are omitted. Last parts of sentences are usually repeated except in the case of Prepositional Phrases, in which case they are omitted. The tendency is to repeat the Subject Noun, main Verb and/or Object Noun.

By obtaining these results we have more evidence of the linguistic competence and limitations of this group of children to bolster the hypotheses formulated from a description of their spontaneous productions. Their analysis of the language they hear seems to be very basic and generalized in nature. Most of their utterances and repetitions can be described as being derived from a limited category set of base structure rules, often context free, which are then translated into generalized phonological rules via conjunction operations. In spontaneous production there is no significant change in the grammatical complexity of utterances produced at age 6 as compared to age 3. On the other hand, grammatical competence *as exhibited in repetition of sentences,* increases over the age range and nearly matches, *but does not exceed* the grammatical competence shown in spontaneous utterances. The grammatical capacity, then, of these children is different from that of normal-speaking children who display in their utterances a deepening analysis of language as an increasingly mature population is observed and who exceed, in some instances, in their repetitions, the grammatical competence displayed in their utterances.

Beyond these findings, some information has been obtained about a general capacity which may lead to the differences in grammatical competence and capacity observed in the normal- and deviant-speaking groups of children. Auditory memory, even for structurally patterned sequences, is much poorer in the deviant-speaking children than in the normal-speaking children. This is especially marked in the youngest child in the group but is even true of the oldest child. Short term memory for even three- to five-morpheme-length utterances was severely limited as indicated by the omissions and modifications of these utterances by all the children in the group. Sixteen of the twenty-seven sentences given for repetition were in this range of length. Twelve of these sixteen sentences were repeated by the 5,11 year old with modifications and omissions. All the remaining utterances which were longer than five morphemes were also repeated with modifications and omissions by this oldest child in the group. There were more omissions and modifications by the younger children in the group. It, therefore, can be stated that short-term memory for and recall of auditory sequences is critically effected by the length of the sequence. This was not the case with normal speaking children. However, the fact that modifications and omissions occurred with three- to five-morpheme-length utterances may be an indication that long-term memory for language, in a specific sense which we will attempt to describe, is effected as well, but not by a mechanism limitation.

It has been postulated that as memory capacity or storage capacity increases, normal-speaking children expand the rules in their grammar, observe more contextual constraints, and, in some instances, reorganize rules to achieve greater definition and economy. These rules are stored in long-term memory for regeneration of various structures. If the 3,0-year-old child could not keep in short-term memory storage more than a two- to three-morpheme-length utterance it is difficult to see how this developing process of a deepening analysis could be carried out, since only a very limited amount of data could be handled at one time. Further, although short-term memory capacity increases over time in this population, it seems that the hypotheses or rules derived from this limited data and to be used in the comprehension and generation of utterances are also limited. If only a limited number of steps in the derivational history of a structure can be stored in long-term memory since short-term memory capacity is limited, then utterances of the type produced by this group of children as well as the type of utterances reproduced would result.

A most extreme case would be that of the deaf child who by definition does not hear these patterned sequences and, therefore, cannot derive and confirm hypotheses from these data and store them in memory. He must laboriously learn to associate visual signs produced by the lips of the speaker to what he himself understands and produces and derive, from this, hypotheses about the language. It would seem, then, that the first step in the generation of utterances by these children would be imitation of a small set of utterances, severely restricted in length (perhaps only one morpheme), and then the derivation of some very limited hypotheses about language.

With these bits of data we have merely begun to explore differences in the capacities of children who acquire language normally and those who do not. As a result of this analysis of their differing linguistic competence a possible basis for these differences has been isolated. In addition, a clue to a necessary factor in normal language acquisition has been obtained. The data are limited by the size of the population and the technique used to elicit information about grammatical competence. This question should be pursued by further experimentation in an exploration of auditory memory capacity of groups of children (both normal and deviant language groups) for nonspeech sequences (this does not mean digits, which are structured phonological sequences often rehearsed), sequences which contain only phonological information (nonsense syllables), and sequences which contain syntactic information of both varying length and complexity. It is important to note that a study of normal language acquisition processes and deviant language acquisition processes and a comparison of the two can give us information about the structure and content of physiological and behavioral processes necessary to language acquisition and use.

Notes

1. An example of this would be to use conditioning techniques which have been found to be successful with the infant to examine his differential responses to speech-sound contrasts as compared to nonspeech-sound differences. The important question in this experimentation is the stimulus comparison, not whether infants can be conditioned using auditory stimuli.
2. It should be stressed that careful planning of stimulus materials is needed since the structure of the question that is asked as well as how it is asked may be critical in determining the validity of the results. For example, if you ask the child to determine which is the plural exemplar and which is the singular exemplar and give him instances such as 'dog digs' and 'dogs dig' you may confuse the issue of whether or not he can make the grammatical judgment because of the phonetic similarity of the instances.
3. For example, C. Fraser, U. Bellugi, and R. Brown, "Control of grammar in imitation, comprehension and production," *J. Verbal Learning Verbal Behavior, 2,* 121-135 (1963).
4. For example, J. Berko, "The child's learning of English morphology," *Word, 14,* 150-177 (1958).
5. P. Menyuk, "A preliminary evaluation of grammatical capacity in children," *J. Verbal Learning Verbal Behavior, 2,* 429-439 (1963); P. Menyuk, "Children's grammatical capacity." In T. Bever and W. Weksel, eds., *The Structure and Psychology of Language* (New York: Holt, Rhinehart and Winston, in press).

6. "She shops and cooks and bakes" can be described as one of the underlying sentences of "She does the shopping and cooking and baking."

7. For exploratory purposes two older children (aged 6,11 years and 8,6 years) and an adult were asked to repeat reverse word order sentences. The older the subject was the greater the number of items that he could repeat. However, even the adult could repeat only about half the items.

8. The conditions of presentation of the reverse word order sentences alters this statement somewhat. These sentences were phrased and therefore were not presented as a word list but rather as grammatical sentences, with stress and intonational contours, might be presented.

9. It seems in these instances and the following instances that the dependent sequential relationships are not being observed in the conjunction construction and that the two sentences are simply being strung together.

10. In the ONS group 'daddy' was frequently substituted for 'Betty' indicating, perhaps, the conformity of the group.

11. The underlined syllable was the stressed syllable both in the presentation of the string and in these kinds of repetitions of the string. The stress pattern and the number of syllables in the string, therefore, were recalled in repetition.

12. See I. Hirsh, "Teaching the deaf child to speak." In F. Smith and G. A. Miller, eds., *The Genesis of Language* (Cambridge, Mass.: The M.I.T. Press, 1966), pp. 207-218, for a brief discussion of how the nature of the hearing loss can affect language acquisition.

13. Systematic variation of stimulus materials in terms of grammaticalness (grammatical, nongrammatical and agrammatical) is an important factor in evaluating children's linguistic comprehension and should be included in experimental tests of linguistic competence, as well as the contrast exemplars, to determine what is understood versus what is produced.

14. P. Menyuk, "Comparison of grammar of children with functionally deviant and normal speech," *J. Speech Hearing Research, 7,* 109-121 (1964).

5 Summary and Conclusions

The following discussion is a summary of the examination of the kinds of rules that may underly the child's production of sentences and, to some extent, the kinds of rules he may be using to comprehend sentences.

5.1 Summary of Developmental Trends Observed

It has been hypothesized that underlying strings formulated by base structure rules contain an element or elements which indicate the application of a transformational operation. In the earliest utterances that are produced this element may be an intonational marker for question, imperative, and declarative sentences. These may be generatively applied to different underlying strings to create different sentence types. The underlying string itself contains only the category 'topic' which can belong to any class in the language (N, V, Prep., Adj., Adv.) plus the intonational marker. A 'topic' can be the negative morpheme ('no') or a question morpheme ('what,' 'where'). The child's concept of 'sentence' may be derived from observations about and production of strings with differing intonational contours. Topics have semantic properties and are entered into the dictionary, at this stage, as either phonetic sequences or phonological features. At the first stage of development the underlying structure of sentences may be as follows:

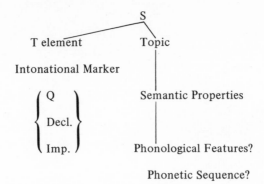

At a somewhat later stage modifiers are sometimes introduced into strings. The relationship expressed in these early utterances is not yet that of Subject and Predicate but Topic and Modifier. Indeed, most of these strings appear to be simply Predicates when one examines the linguistic context in which they are produced. By use of these few rules various sentence types can be generated.

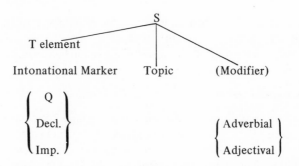

The child cannot convey the specific relation of a negative and a topic or the content of a specific question by the application of stress or intonational rules. These latter rules may convey the difference between '(give me) another horsie!,' '(that's) another horsie' and '(Is it) another horsie?' but not the difference between 'Where's another horsie?' and '(Is it) another horsie?' or the difference between 'That's another horsie' and 'That's not another horsie.' One might hypothesize, then, that expansion of syntactic rules is motivated by the need to convey more specific meaning. However, until the child has the competence to derive rules which he can use to generate utterances which convey more specific meaning he does not do so.[1]

In the production of declarative, question and negative sentences, at a later stage of development, a change in the generation of these sentence types can be observed. The T element is expanded into some morpheme (NP, no, not, what, where) and conjoined to the underlying string to create various sentence types.

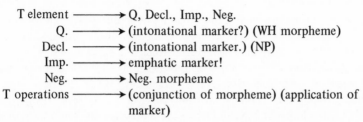

> T element ⟶ Q, Decl., Imp., Neg.
> Q. ⟶ (intonational marker?) (WH morpheme)
> Decl. ⟶ (intonational marker.) (NP)
> Imp. ⟶ emphatic marker!
> Neg. ⟶ Neg. morpheme
> T operations ⟶ (conjunction of morpheme) (application of marker)

Both conjunction of morpheme and then application of marker can be applied to the underlying strings in some instances. Thus declarative sentences with question intonation are produced ("write name, mommy?") and negative sentences with emphatic stress are produced ("no touch!" and "no do!"), but WH-morpheme sentences with question intonation are not produced.

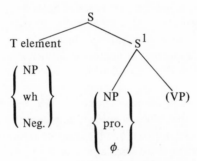

There are some restrictions on the conjoining of elements that are observed. The NP of S is equal to or related to the NP (pro) of S^1 and there are restrictions on the occurrence of the WH morpheme of S and the Verb of S^1. There seem to be no evident restrictions on the conjunction of Neg. and S^1.

By using these rules the child achieves greater definition of context. He achieves the contrasts 'touch it' and 'no touch it,' 'that car' and 'no car,' 'there hat' and 'where hat?' and 'daddy do' and 'what daddy do?'

It has been hypothesized that the child begins to use transformational rules after using only base structure rules to achieve greater economy in language generation. He may have, at some stage in his grammatical development, several types of rules to generate a sentence type. He, therefore, reduces memory strain by reducing the total number of rules needed to generate various forms of a sentence type.[2] This is a logical explanation and is the basis for postulating the use of a generative grammar with productive rules rather than memorization of instances or types of instances. However, although the child seems to be producing types of utterances in accordance with rules that are quite different from those that are postulated to be used to generate completely well-formed structures, one can observe that he seems to be using the same types of rules to generate all these sentence types at the beginning stages of sentence usage and again at somewhat later stages of sentence usage. There is a great savings in the total grammar in using this device. At some overlapping stages of development the child may have more than one set of rules in his grammar for generating the same structure and, thus, it may be hypothesized that he has more rules than does the adult for generating the same type of structure. However, he hasn't yet acquired the complete set of rules to generate these structures, so that his total number of rules may be smaller.

Rather than hypothesizing a passive model of acquisition in which the child is pushed into acquiring new types of rules by 'memory strain' or a 'need for greater definition' what seems to be occurring is an active change in the structures used dependent on changes in the basic mechanisms underlying the child's increasing competence (increasing memory capacity, for one) and based on previous acquisitions. All instances cited as evidence of transformational use are dependent on the development of the auxiliary/modal node in the base structure rules, and, therefore represent the development of the child's linguistic competence to the point where he is using, for the most part, the complete set of rules for the derivation of sentence types specific to his language. This development is dependent on further expansions of a base structure rule.

These observations about the sentences that are produced lead one to the conclusion that the base component of the grammar, at its earliest stages of development, contains elements which indicate which transformations will apply and rules for their application. These rules, at first, are applications of intonation and stress patterns and then, somewhat later, conjunction of a morpheme to a string plus the application of intonation and stress patterns.

There have been questions asked and statements made about whether or not the child, in his order of acquisition of structures, follows the order postulated for the derivation of certain structures. The utterances produced at an early stage of development indicate that this is not the case.

Children's early sentences can be described as expressing syntactic relationships not specific to their language and categorial component and combinational rules which, to some degree, defy the rules specific to their language. The lexical items in the string have some semantic properties. There is some element in the base component that indicates the application of intonation and stress or the addition of a morpheme. To these derived strings, phonological rules may be applied. The base component rules and structures are incomplete, semantic properties are limited, the transformational rules are also incomplete, and the phonological rules are far from being completely developed.[3] Therefore, the obvious answer to the question of 'same ordering' in acquisition as in derivation is 'no.' The child proceeds from different, minimal, and generalized base structure rules to generalized and minimal transformational rules to probably different, minimal, and generalized phonological rules to output.[4] If the order of derivation of utterances was followed in the acquisition of structures, we would observe completely developed base component rules, then completely developed transformational rules, and then completely developed phonological rules.

One might then state that the child's generation of a string (or order of acquisition of structures) is in the same order as those postulated for the derivation of a completely well-formed structure, but with pieces missing. We note the child filling in the skeletal frame of his base component rules, acquiring more transformational rules and refining his phonological rules. This statement is incorrect since at the acquisition stages of development the child's grammar can be described as being different from the postulated description of the grammar of the language not only in number of rules but in the *kinds* of rules used to derive semantically alike sentences (for example, the development from 'No boy' to 'That not boy' to 'That's not some boy' to 'That's not a boy'). The kinds of rules used by the child to derive these structures seem very much dependent on his level of competence in dealing with linguistic generalizations at various stages of development. The structure of the rules used to derive these semantically alike sentence types changes, in systematic ways, over the developmental period until completely well-formed instances of sentence types occur.

The grammatical operations the child can perform on strings (add, invert, substitute, embed, observe selectional constraints 1, 2, etc.) are reflections of various levels of syntactic competence. The changes that one observes in the child's use of these grammatical operations in the generation of sentences over a developmental period seem to be indications of the child's capacity to acquire a symbol system of the structure Grammar without directed instruction. Knowledge of whether one sentence type appears before another in a child's language use is not very informative, especially given the population size in studies of syntax acquisition. However, knowledge of the operations the child uses to derive these sentence types is most informative. One observes that once a basic operation needed to generate a form of a sentence type is used, this same operation is applied in the generation of other sentence types. This, in fact, may be the explanation for the observation that various structures appear in language production almost simultaneously. Others may lag because additional operations or other kinds of operations are needed for their generation.

To summarize, the child in the production of early sentences seems capable of the following operations: He can conjoin a topic and a modifier and create different sentence types by the application of rules for intonation and stress to the base structure string. He can expand an element into a morpheme and conjoin a morpheme to the base structure string. Some selectional restrictions on the cooccurrence of the morpheme and the string are observed. The morpheme is then embedded in the string and syntactic restrictions are observed concerning the placement of the morpheme within the sentence. In addition to the above, there are structures which are probably memorized and produced in the string with no fully developed underlying structure such as "I'm," "It's," "He's" (no Aux underlying structure); "wanna," "gonna" (no underlying infinitival complement structure); "came" (no Verb + past tense underlying structure).

While the child is beginning to use types of rules for the generation of various kinds of sentences, he is also changing and expanding rules in the base component of the grammar. He establishes the Subject-Predicate relationship in his sentences and begins to define the classes in the language. As he establishes this relationship and begins to define classes he also, at this stage of development, expands the nodes in the tree structure of his sentences. The nature of his transformational rules changes. He begins to permute items and attach items to each other. However, until the classes Auxiliary/Modal and tense are established, instances of completely well-formed declarative, question and negative sentences are not observed. The interdependency of base structure and transformational rules is evident.

The child not only has to acquire the Subject-Predicate relationship in his sentences, define and establish the classes in his language and acquire rules for addition, deletion, substitution, and permutation of items in a string; he must also observe contextual constraints on the cooccurrence of members of classes in a string. Although most of these basic tasks seem to have been accomplished by about age 4 by the children in this population, the last task is not accomplished by this age. As the child's lexicon and base structure rules expand he must observe more and different contextual constraints that may be operating over longer and longer sequences. An important aspect of grammatical development, after this period, is closer and closer approximations to completely well-formed rules for the generation of particular structures as an increasingly older population is observed. Examples of this kind of behavior can be observed in the use of base structure rules and morphological rules. Grossly, sentences are being generated with varying degrees of differentiation at various stages of development, and this is largely the result of additions in syntactic properties and additions in observation of rules of cooccurrence or selectional restrictions.

The outstanding developments that occur in the sentences that children produce over the age range of approximately 4 to 7 years are (1) further expansion of base structure nodes (increase in class membership, (2) observation of selectional constraints on the cooccurrence of members of a class (observation of syntactic properties and combinatorial rules of lexical items), and (3) application of the syntactic operations of addition, deletion, substitution, and permutation to underlying sentences, as well as to items in a single underlying string. These developments probably continue well beyond age 7.

One other aspect of increasing grammatical competence is gradual elimination of the generation of various transformational structures with incomplete rules and then elimination of the generation of structures with generalizations about rules. However, as new types of transformational structures are acquired there are productions of these structures which seem to be generated by approximations to the complete set of rules needed to generate that structure. Older children, however, as they acquire a new structure seem to apply generalizations about rules to this new structure rather than simply omitting rules.

A diagramed statement of these observations would be as follows:

Branching   *Further Branching*

Transformational Operations   *Changes in Transformational Operations*

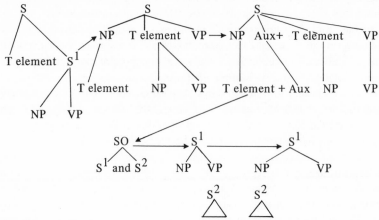

Properties and Rules of Cooccurrence   *Addition of Properties and Rules*
                                          of Cooccurrence

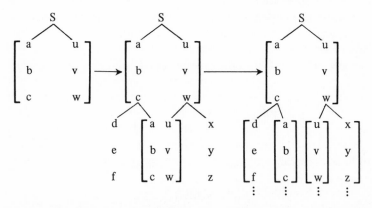

Changes in branching, transformational operations and additions in properties and rules of cooccurrence are, of course, all occurring simultaneously.

5.2 Hypotheses about Possible Relationships to Psychological Mechanisms

Descriptions of the sentences children produce at various stages of development lead to certain hypotheses about the linguistic processes that occur in the acquisition of grammar. Some of these hypotheses are the following:

1. The child can determine the linguistically significant generalizations or categories in his acoustic environment. For example, he can determine what a 'sentence' is, what a 'word' is and what a 'speech sound' is.

2. The child can store in memory the features of these categories. For example, in the case of 'sentence,' he notes a sequence with a falling intonational contour and, later, that such a sequence contains the structures NP and VP. He can generate utterances containing these features.

3. The child can store in memory the functional relationships of these features. He can identify and label the difference between falling and rising intonational contours. He stores the fact that NP of 'sentence' is the 'Subject,' and NP of VP is the 'Object.'

4. The child adds to the properties of the members of these categories. Falling intonational contour is Decl., Neg., WH morpheme Q, and rising intonation contour is Aux Inversion Q, Decl. Q, Neg. Q[5]. A Noun is human, male, singular, etc.

5. The child can determine the fit and structure of sequences he produces and hears. S_1 is a 'sentence,' S_2 is partially a sentence,[6] and S_3 is not a sentence.

6. The child can both expand and alter his structural descriptions of these categories, classes, and properties to more closely approximate the structural descriptions in the grammar of his language as he matures. He can generate utterances from these altered descriptions.

These hypotheses are based on descriptions of the sentences children produce. Such a description may logically eliminate some theoretical models of language acquisition because of their inadequacy in accounting for what must be acquired—the grammar of the language. It presupposes that the child has the capacity (1) to perceive and identify abstract features in the linguistic data that he hears, (2) to store these features and descriptions of possible manipulations of these features in memory in a retrievable form, (3) to apply these descriptions to each utterance he generates and hears to come to some realization or determination of a sentence, and (4) to add and reorganize this information in the light of what he already knows and what he continues to find in the linguistic data.

Evidence for deriving the above hypotheses about the child's grammatical competence at various stages of development and his grammatical capacity are, as was stated, descriptions of the sentences children produce and what they do not produce (that is, imitations of increasing bits of sentences). However, there are many problems and large areas of question associated with describing what is produced and considering these descriptions to be a description of the child's level of grammatical competence or a reflection of the child's capacity to acquire a language.

The study comparing children's performance in spontaneously producing sentences and their performance in reproducing sentences indicates that the following might be said of structural descriptions of their competence based on the sentences they produce. For the most part, children's reproduction of structures is limited by the rules that have been described to be in their grammar, since they often reproduce sentences with the structural descriptions found in their production rather than those in the sentences given. In this sense, structural descriptions of the utterances they produce seem to be an accurate representation of their grammatical competence. In certain instances, when given the memory aid of a sentence to repeat, children exceed the level of competence displayed in their spontaneous productions. However, these are always instances of structures which they are probably in the process of acquiring, since they appear in the spontaneous productions of children that are a little older. Therefore, structural descriptions of the sentences children produce may lag somewhat behind the child's level of competence in comprehending syntactic structures, but not too far behind. The observation that the number of rules (expansion) and type of rules (transformational operations) in children's grammar changes over the age range is supported by the fact that sentences are reproduced with certain types of modifications at various ages reflecting these changes in number and types of rules.

The children's reproduciton of nongrammatical utterances indicates that descriptions of the nongrammatical productions is, in many instances, a description of rules used for the generation of sentences rather than a description of children's grammatical competence. The results of the reproduction task indicate that in producing a sentence, although the set of rules for a structure has been acquired, children sometimes do not use the complete set of rules, since, in repetition, they may either spontaneously correct a nongrammatical structure or correct a nongrammatical structure when asked to do so. Nevertheless, in terms of formulation of a model of the linguistic performance of children at various stages of development, the differences in production and comprehension are important.

From the results of both structural descriptions of the sentences children produce and structural descriptions of the sentences they reproduce one might hypothesize that the child's procedure in understanding and generating utterances and in changing the level of his competence in understanding and generating utterances is the following:

1. He acquires some rules to understand and reproduce sentences.

2. Using the rules of his grammar he samples the utterance and by some matching procedures he determines the structural description of the utterance.

3. Using the rules of his grammar he generates an utterance but sometimes does not complete the order of rules needed to generate the completely well-formed structure.

4. He stores the rules of his grammar but only has enough computing space or memory to store a subset of the rules of the grammar of his language.

5. The set of rules of his grammar is expanded when computing space increases (number of rules increases) and when computing space is reorganized (additional restrictions, types of properties of lexical items, types of operations).

The role of memory in language acquisition has been emphasized. The complete structure of that role is not clear. In the comparison of the spontaneous productions and reproductions of children who were producing language in a deviant manner it was found that these children performed in some instances at a much more immature level of competence and in other instances in a different manner (such as only last words) in their reproduction of sentences than in their spontaneous production of sentences. Children using normal language, on the other hand, exceed, in some instances, the level of competence represented in spontaneous production. If the sampling procedure of the children using deviant language is severely limited (and, therefore, possibly distorted), as indicated in their reproductions, then the structural descriptions in their grammar would not change rapidly and some of these structural descriptions would be quite different from those of normal-speaking children. We observe both phenomena occurring in their spontaneous productions. The type of structural descriptions in their grammar does not change markedly over an age range of 3 years as do those of normal-speaking children, and some of these descriptions are different from those of normal-speaking children. However, the problem does not seem to be simply more limited storage capacity. They seem to be able to store the rules that they acquire and retrieve them for use in spontaneously generating utterances. A tentative hypothesis, then, would be that the difficulty lies in short-term memory capacity or the perceptual devices that are used. To derive the rules that are acquired, many more samplings of the data would be needed. This would take a longer period of time and in some instances the rules would be distorted. As a result of this study, the question of the pattern of development of perceptual devices combined with storage capacity and the role this developing pattern plays in normal language acquisition is raised. Structural descriptions of the sentences produced and reproduced by children using deviant language not only can clarify the problem of these children in acquiring language but can also point to critical factors in the normal acquisition of language.

5.3   Some Further Questions

The primary emphasis in this discussion has been structural descriptions of the utterances children produce. By examining the linguistic descriptions of these utterances an attempt has been made to determine the changes in grammatical operations the child seems capable of performing in the production of these sentences over time. It has been indicated that only a description of the underlying structure of children's utterances can lead to a determination of the stages of developing grammatical competence and performance, and that these descriptions should identify operations and their order of acquisition rather than provide an ordered list of labeled structures. Such a description indicates certain developmental trends and can operationally define the content of these developmental trends, rather than simply stating that language becomes more complex or sentences longer over time. It can also give us clues to the psychological processes which may be involved in grammar acquisition and development.

The description of the language children produce during these stages of development is far from complete. This is especially true of the phonological and semantic components of children's grammar where descriptions have been, thus far, either observational or fragmentary. The use of prosodic features at the earliest stages of development falls into this category. The very interesting question of the relationship between morphological rules and phonological rules has yet to be systematically explored. The hierarchy of acquisition of semantic properties and the process of semantic differentiation of properties have yet to be examined. The conditions of early lexical item acquisition (the effect of situation context or syntactic context) should be studied experimentally. The early or late acquisition of certain syntactic structures has not been completely explained. Grammatical complexity on a comparative basis between structure and structure has not been fully described. Both aspects, number of rules needed to derive a structure and types of rules (selectional restrictions, properties of lexical items, types of operations, etc.), operate simultaneously in the generation of sentences. These aspects need to be parcelled out in experimental situations.

Not only are descriptions of spontaneous productions (perhaps the easiest data to collect if not to analyze) far from complete, but in the areas of perception and comprehension the data are almost totally lacking. In order to substantiate or perhaps modify hypotheses about grammar acquisition these data are necessary. One must systematically explore how utterances are comprehended (that is, as we structurally describe them or otherwise) and how the structure of this comprehension changes over time. There is some evidence that, on the whole, the child does not produce what he does not comprehend, but these data are quite limited both in terms of structures examined and in terms of age range (approximately 3 to 6 years). Not only will this research enable us to test hypotheses, it will add greatly to our body of knowledge about the 'facts' of language acquisition and development. This knowledge, in turn, will give us further information about the behavioral and, hopefully, physiological functioning of an organism that acquires language.

The relationships between the capacities exhibited and the procedures used by the child to acquire the grammar of his language and the capacities and procedures used in the acquisition of other abstract systems have yet to be explored. During the language acquisition period the child achieves the ability to add together, delete, substitute, and invert items to generate new strings. He must observe restrictions concerned with specific context. He achieves the ability to observe sentence X and sentence Y and determine that their underlying structure is the same or different and in what ways they are the same or different. In the acquisition of other abstract perceptual and conceptual systems he must be able to perform similar operations. In language acquisition the child achieves this competence although he is exposed to only a minimal amount of possible data which may often contain a great deal of noise. This may be true of the acquisition of other abstract systems as well. Some comparative questions might be put about possible similarities between linguistic and other cognitive operations such as: Does the child achieve the ability to identify, differentiate, reject various stimulus inputs from a small amount of possible data? Can one observe a developmental hierarchy (ordered and dependent)? Are these operations maturationally determined?

Throughout this discussion the similarities between children in syntax development at various stages have been noted. Logically, this approach is necessary since the first task is to understand how all children may proceed in acquiring language. We may then be able to describe the basic processes, both physiological and psychological, involved in language acquisition. These descriptions can provide the bases for describing and possibly explaining differences between children in their use of language as a cognitive and social tool. Those interested primarily in children's language acquisition and development per se will be interested in answers to such questions as: What factors cause a child's use of language to be considered as different? How different is it? Why is it different? All are of vital importance.

Notes

1. The possible underlying basis of this increasing competence will be discussed in the next section.
2. D. McNeill, "Developmental Psycholinguistics," Mimeo, Center for Cognitive Studies, Harvard University, 1965.
3. It has been indicated that mastery of articulation normally does not take place until age 7 or 8. See M. H. Powers, "Functional disorders of articulation—symptomatology and etiology." In L. E. Travis, ed., *Handbook of Speech Pathology* (New York: Appleton-Century-Crofts, 1957).
4. The stages of development in the acquisition of the phonological component are analogous to those observed in the development of the syntactic component. Nonexpansion of a symbol, nonobservation of selectional restrictions and further expansion of a terminal symbol can be observed in phonological development (P. Menyuk, *Language Development* (Text in series entitled *Current Research in Developmental Psychology*, J. C. Wright, ed., [Englewood Cliffs, N.J.: Prentice-Hall, in Preparation])).
5. The symbols Decl., Neg., Q are used in place of the structural descriptions (that is, $S \rightarrow Neg. + S_1$) of these sentence types at various stages of development.
6. S_2 may be nongrammatical or anomalous.

References

Ammons, R. B. and H. S. Ammons. *Full Range Picture Vocabulary* (Missoula, Montana: Psychological Test Specialists, 1958).

Bellugi, U. and R. Brown, eds. *The Acquisition of Language* (Monographs of the Society for Research in Child Development, No. 29 (1964).

Berko, Jean. "The child's learning of English morphology," *Word, 14,* 150-177 (1958).

Bever, T. G., J. A. Fodor, and W. Weksel. "On the acquisition of syntax: A critique of 'contextual generalization,' " *Psychol. Rev., 72,* 467-482 (1965).

Blum, G. S. *The Blacky Pictures: A Technique for Exploration of Personality Dynamics,* Manual (New York: Psychological Corp., 1950).

Brain, R. "The neurology of language," *Brain, 84,* 145-163 (1961).

Braine, M. D. S. "The ontogeny of English phrase structure," *Language, 39,* 1-13 (1963).

_____. "On learning the grammatical order of words," *Psychol. Rev., 70,* 323-340 (1963).

Chomsky, N. "The general properties of language." In F. L. Darley, ed., *Brain Mechanisms underlying Speech and Language* (New York: Grune and Stratton, 1967), pp. 93-98.

_____. *Aspects of the Theory of Syntax* (Cambridge, Mass.: The M.I.T. Press, 1965).

Davis, H., S. K. Hirsh, J. Shelnutt, and C. Bowers. "Further validation of evoked response audiometry (ERA)," *J. Speech Hearing Research, 10,* 717-721 (1967).

Dollard, J. and N. E. Miller. *Personality and Psychotherapy* (New York: McGraw-Hill, 1950).

Ervin, S. "Structure in children's language." Paper presented at International Congress of Psychology, Washington, D.C., 1963.

Flavell, J. H. *The Developmental Psychology of Jean Piaget* (New York: Van Nostrand, 1963).

Fodor, J. and M. Garret. "Some reflections on competence and performance." In J. Lyons and R. J. Wales, eds., *Psycholingustics Papers* (Chicago: Aldine, 1966), pp. 135-154.

159

Fodor, J. and T. G. Bever. "The psychological reality of linguistic segments," *J. Verbal Learning Verbal Behavior, 4,* 414-420 (1965).

Fraser, C., U. Bellugi, and R. Brown. "Control of grammar in imitation, comprehension and production," *J. Verbal Learning Verbal Behavior, 2,* 121-135 (1963).

Friedlander, B. Z. "The effect of speaker identity, inflection, vocabulary and message redundancy on infants' selection of vocal reinforcers." Paper presented at Society for Research in Child Development, March, 1967.

Greenberg, J. H. "Some universals of grammar with particular reference to the order of meaningful elements." In J. H. Greenberg, ed., *Universals of Language* (Cambridge, Mass.: The M.I.T. Press, 1963), pp. 58-85.

Gruber, J. "Topicalization in child language." Mimeo, M.I.T. Modern Languages Dept., March 29, 1966.

Halle, M. and K. Stevens. "Speech recognition: a model and a program for research," *I.R.E. Trans. Inform. Theory, I,* 1-8 (1962).

————. "On the role of simplicity in linguistic descriptions." American Mathematical Society, *Proceedings of Symposia in Applied Mathematics: Structure of Language and its Mathematical Aspects, 12,* 89-94 (1961).

————. "Questions of linguistics." *N. 2 del supplemento al Vol. 13,* Serie X, del Nuovo Amento, 494-517 (1959).

Hirsh, I. "Teaching the deaf child to speak." In F. Smith and G. A. Miller, eds., *The Genesis of Language* (Cambridge, Mass.: The M. I. T. Press, 1966), pp. 207-218.

Hubel, D. H. and T. N. Wiesel. "Receptive fields, binocular interaction and functional architecture in the cat's visual cortex," *J. Physiol., 160,* 106-154 (1962).

Inhelder, B. and J. Piaget. *The Growth of Logical Thinking from Childhood to Adolescence* (New York: Basic Books, 1958).

Institute of Child Welfare. *The Minnesota Scale for Parental Occupation* (Minneapolis: University of Minnesota, 1950).

Irvin, O. C. "Infant speech: The effect of family occupational status and of age on use of sound types" *J. Speech Disorders, 13,* 31-34 (1948).

————. "Infant speech: The effect of family occupational status and of age on sound frequency," *J. Speech Disorders, 13,* 320-323 (1948).

Jakobson, R. "Towards a linguistic typology of aphasia." In *Disorders of Language,* Ciba Foundation Symposium (Boston: Little Brown, 1964), pp. 2-42.

————. "Implication of language universals for linguistics." In J. H. Grunberg, ed., *Universals of Language* (Cambridge, Mass.: The M.I.T. Press, 1963), pp. 208-219.

Jenkins, J. and D. S. Palermo. "Mediation processes and the acquisition of linguisitc structure." In U. Bellugi and R. Brown, eds. *The Acquisition of Language* (Monographs of the Society for Research in Child Development, No. 92, 1964), pp. 141-169.

Kagan, J. and M. Lewis. "Studies of Attention in the Human Infant," *Merrill-Palmer Quarterly, 2* (1965), pp. 95-127.

Katz, J. J. and J. A. Fodor. "The structure of a semantic theory." In J. A. Fodor and J. J. Katz, *The Structure of Language* (Englewood Cliffs, N. J.: Prentice Hall, 1964), pp. 479-518.

————. and P. M. Postal. *An Integrated Theory of Linguistic Descriptions.* (Cambridge, Mass.: The M.I.T. Press, 1964).

Kimura, D. "Cerebral dominance and perception of verbal stimuli," *Canad. J. Psychol., 15,* 166-171 (1961).

Klima, E. S. and U. Bellugi. "Syntactic regularities in the speech of children." In J. Lyons and R. J. Wales, eds., *Psycholinguistics Papers* (Chicago: Aldine, 1966), pp. 183-208.

Lenneberg, E. H. "The natural history of language." In F. Smith and G. A. Miller, eds., *Genesis of Language* (Cambridge, Mass.: The M.I.T. Press, 1966).

————. "Speech development: Its anatomical and physiological concomitants." In E. C. Carterette, ed., *Brain Function, Vol. III Speech, Language, and Communication* (Berkeley, Calif.: University of California Press, 1966), pp. 37-66.

Lieberman, P. *Intonation, Perception and Language* (Cambridge, Mass.: The M.I.T. Press, 1967).

———. "On the acoustic basis of the perception of intonation by linguists," *Word, 21,* 40-53 (1965).

Lipsitt, L. P. "Learning in the first year of life." In L. P. Lipsitt and C. C. Spiker, eds., *Advances in Child Development and Behavior* (New York: Academic Press, 1963), pp. 147-196.

Luria, A. R. "Factors and forms of aphasia." In *Disorders of Language,* Ciba Foundation Symposium (Boston: Little Brown, 1964), pp. 112-167.

Matthews, G. H. "Analysis by synthesis of sentences of natural languages" (London: National Physics Laboratory Symposium, No. 13, 1961), pp. 531-543.

McCarthy, D. "Language development in children." In L. Carmichael, ed., *Manual of Child Psychology* (New York: Wiley, 1954), pp. 492-630.

———. *Language Development of the Pre-School Child* (Minneapolis: University of Minnesota Press, 1930).

McNeill, D. "Developmental psycholinguistics." In I. Smith and G. A. Miller, eds., *Genesis of Language* (Cambridge, Mass.: The M.I.T. Press, 1966), pp. 15-84.

———. "Developmental Psycholinguistics." Mimeo, Center for Cognitive Studies, Harvard University, 1965.

Mehler, J. "Some effects of grammatical transformations on the recall of English sentences." *J. Verbal Learning Verbal Behavior, 2,* 346-351 (1963).

Menyuk, P. *Language Development* (Text in series entitled *Current Research in Developmental Psychology,* J. C. Wright, ed., Prentice-Hall, in preparation).

———. "Children's grammatical capacity." In T. G. Bever and W. Weksel, eds., *The Structure and Psychology of Language* (New York: Holt, Rhinehart and Winston, in press).

———. "The role of distinctive features in children's acquisition of phonology" *J. Speech Hearing Research, 11,* 138-146 (1968).

———. "Comparison of grammar of children with functionally deviant and normal speech." *J. Speech Hearing Research, 7,* 109-121 (1964).

———. "Alternation of rules in children's grammar," *J. Verbal Learning Verbal Behavior, 3,* 480-488 (1964).

———. "A preliminary evaluation of grammatical capacity in children," *J. Verbal Learning Verbal Behavior, 2,* 429-439 (1963).

———. "Syntactic structures in the language of children," *J. Child Develop., 34,* 407-422 (1963).

Miller, G. A. and N. Chomsky. "Finitary models of language users." In D. Luce, R. Bush, and E. Gallanter, eds., *Handbook of Mathematical Psychology, Vol. III* (New York: Wiley, 1963), pp. 419-492.

Miller, W. R. "The acquisition of grammatical rules by children." Paper presented at Linguistic Society of America Annual Meeting, December, 1964.

Mowrer, O. H. "Hearing and speaking: an analysis of language learning," *J. Speech Hearing Disorders, 23,* 143-153 (1960).

Murai, J. J. "Speech development of infants." *Psychologia III,* No. 1, 29-35 (1960).

Museyibova, T. A. "The development of the understanding of spatial relations and their reflection in the language of children of pre-school age." In B. G. Anan'yev and B. F. Lomov, eds., *Problem of Spatial Perception and Spatial Concepts* (Washington D.C.: NASA, NASA Technical Translation, June 1964).

Palermo, D. S. "On learning to talk." *Research Bulletin No. 61,* Dept. of Psychology, Pennsylvania State University, Feb. 1966.

Powers, M. H. "Functional disorders of articulation—symptomatology and etiology." In L. E. Travis, ed., *Handbook of Speech Pathology* (New York: Appleton-Century-Crofts, 1957).

Rheingold, H. L., *et al.,* "Social conditioning of vocalizations in the infant," *J. Comp. Physiol. Psych., 52* (1959).

Rosenberg, P. S. "Phrase structure principles of English complex sentence formation," *J. Linguistics, 3,* 103-118 (1967).

Saussure, Ferdinand de. *Course in General Linguistics,* C. Bally and A. Sechehaye, eds. (New York: Philosophical Library. 1959).

Savin, H. B. and E. Perchonock. "Grammatical structure and immediate recall of English sentences," *J. Verbal Learning Verbal Behavior, 4,* 348-353 (1965).

Shankweiler, D. "Effects of temporal lobe damage on perception of dichotically presented melodies," *J. Comp. Physiol. Psychol., 62,* 115-119 (1966).

Stokoe, W. C. *Sign Language Structure: An Outline of Visual Communication Systems of the American Deaf* (Washington, D.C.: Gallaudet College, 1960).

Wales, R. J. and J. C. Marshall. "The organization of linguistic performance." In J. Lyons and J. R. Wales, eds., *Psycholinguistics Papers* (Chicago: Aldine, 1966), pp. 29-80.

Weir, Ruth. *Language in the Crib* (The Hague: Mouton and Co., 1962).

Wickelgren, W. A. "Distinctive features and errors in short-term memory for English consonants," *J. Acoust. Soc. Am., 39,* 388-398 (1966).

————. "Distinctive features and errors in short-term memory for English vowels," *J. Acoust. Soc. Am., 38,* 583-588 (1965).

Vygotsky, L. A. *Thought and Language* (Cambridge, Mass.: The M.I.T. Press, 1962).

Index